To a successful
Life

YOUR PRACTICE BY DESIGN...

A Step by Step Guide to being a High Performance Insurance Broker.

By Mike & Maria Keiser

This book is dedicated to our children Morgann & Evan,
who have patiently stuck with us through all of our entrepreneurial ventures.
Thank you for your listening, input and your willingness to jump in when we needed you.

Thank you for purchasing this book

Sign up for our mailing list to receive special updates, offers, and access to bonus content. Including help with the exercises.

http://mentalcompass.com/your-practice/

Copyright

First published in the United States of America in 2013 by Mike & Maria Keiser. Edited by Mary Chizeck.

Artwork by Marijana Marinkovic

Pictures by Alisha Martindale

Legalese

The information contained in this guide is for informational purposes only.

The material may include information, products, or services by third parties. As such, we do not assume responsibility or liability for any third party material or opinions.

First edition, November 2013.

You may find different pathways to success for your business—great! We hope you'll consider sharing your success story with us at info@theecircle.com.

Happy reading!

TABLE OF CONTENTS

RESOURCES

INTRODUCTION

As you might have already guessed, this isn't a book about cooking, bird watching, football, or stamp collecting, although those are all fine topics. No, this book serves one purpose. It's about as straight forward as you can get. No matter if you are a relative rookie in the insurance business or a seasoned veteran, this book is for any broker who wants to reach the upper levels of their field. It's written for the proactive broker who believes in the concept of "working on" their business and wants to be their very best. The principles that we'll discuss here are applicable to every type of insurance broker with every type of experience. Our goal is to help brokers create and implement a roadmap and examine their practice in a way they never have before. You'll see yourself and your business in a whole new way if you commit to applying the principles that we'll be talking about. We're going to offer you a system for becoming your best self. We've seen people grow their revenue by more than 300% over 3 years. We've seen people increase their profit margins, reduce their costs, and enjoy what they do much more. What we're going to talk about isn't some "pie in the sky" mumbo jumbo. This is real world, applicable principles that simply require your commitment and effort. As we like to say, simple doesn't always mean easy. But this is a simple set of tools that can and will have a dramatic effect on your results.

There are a couple of things that this book is not. It isn't a book on how to sell better. We'll leave that to sales experts. You may discover on your journey to peak performance that your sales skills are an issue. If they are, address it. If they aren't an issue, don't worry about it. But it's not a book on how to sell or market better. It's also not a book about positive thinking, although positive psychology plays a major role in our principles. It's not really a management book either. Well…then what the heck is it? We'd be happy to tell you if we had any idea ourselves. Seriously, it is the culmination of 10 years of working with insurance brokers and general agents. We've gotten to understand how you folks think, how you approach your business, your preferred methods of communication, and your keys to success. In saying that it's not a sales book or a management book, we won't be teaching you any "techniques" here. Instead, we'll be showing you a system and a way of thinking, managing your mind, communicating, and managing your behavior that will lead to much greater results than you've ever had. How do we know this? The reason is because we see it every day. So what makes us so darn smart and qualifies us to write such a book? Although neither one of us has a PhD from Wharton or any such thing, we have been working with business owners (in particular, insurance brokers) with huge results for over 10 years.

We've been offering peer advisory boards, executive coaching, and peak performance training to business owners, executives, and advisors of all different types. We even do some corporate executive coaching for companies like Aetna and Stanley, Black, & Decker. In addition to the work we've done with business owners, we've also been doing a great deal of research for more than 6 years. We've interviewed psychologists, psychiatrists, entrepreneurs, athletes, athletic coaches, and studied a number of university research papers on human performance, human behavior, positive psychology, and entrepreneurship. We've also practiced everything on ourselves. Every principle that we discuss is something that we've vetted, practiced, and proven. It was vitally important to us to only present you with information and ideas that are real and usable. Even though we've worked with many different industries, our real passion is with insurance brokers. We find you particularly enjoyable to work with and extremely willing to do what it takes to be your best. We've also had our greatest results with brokers. We continue to tweak our programs and principles to meet the needs of advisors who want to reach the upper echelon of their ability. Thank you for being so cool to work with.

Some of what we talk about you will have heard before. That's why we sometimes refer to our programs as "ancient wisdom combined with the science and technology of modern man". You hear certain things a lot because they are true. And we can't stress enough, we will only ever present you with ideas that are proven and actually work. Nothing you're going to read is based on theory. It has been tested and retested. We had no intention of putting out a book until we were certain people would get results from it.

We realize that you'll find this book amazingly entertaining and useful, which is going to make you want to read the whole thing in one sitting. We get it. But please don't. This book will serve you much better if you savor every morsel. We'd like you to go through each chapter and understand how it applies to you and what actions you should take. Really dig into each chapter. Use a journal if you need to. Mark up the pages. But make it personal to you. Don't just read the words. Use them. We've arranged the book so that each chapter builds upon the other. Also, be honest with yourself about where you are and where you'd like to be. Sometimes taking a hard look in the mirror can be very challenging. It's a tough pill to swallow when we realize we're the problem. The good news is that everyone has the potential to be a peak performer, to be better than they were the day before. That's all we're asking...just be a little better today than you were yesterday. If you follow that philosophy, you'll be amazed at the speed and efficiency with which you improve, even if you're pretty awesome already.

We understand that some people are surely going to be asking, "why does the insurance industry need another book on how to be better, faster, wiser, and more successful? Fair question. What makes our self help any better than anyone else's self help? We think there are plenty of reasons. But if you are someone who likes a little more detail, here's why we think everyone should read this book. First, as we mentioned above, it's all based on research and practice. Much of the material we've found in the self help world is based on theory or fads. Some of it just dreamed up out of thin air with no real basis in fact or application. We've also been at this for over 10 years and have seen exactly what has made some brokers wildly successful while some just muddle through. We work with real people who have real insurance practices. Finally, we've been working on ourselves all along too; since we began applying these principles to our own business, we've increased our revenues by 25% per year. This is also our passion. Just like some people dreamed of being rock stars or astronauts when they grew up, we dreamed of coaching and consulting to insurance brokers. The work we do is very satisfying and we were just looking for a way to get this information to more people.

We wish you the best of luck on your endeavor to be your best. It's not always easy but it will be something that you'll be happy you engaged in. People we've worked with feel a true sense of accomplishment as they see the improvements start to take place, when they see their hard work paying off. The biggest message we want to have you start the book off with is that it's possible for you too. It's all within you. We're just here to help draw some more of it out. So, have fun, take your time, and just know that elite performance is well within your reach. Now...please allow us to share some stories and bits of wisdom that will help you create a high performing insurance practice.

CHAPTER 1 – WHAT THE HECK IS PEAK PERFORMANCE ANYWAY (AND WHY SHOULD YOU CARE)?

Scary term, isn't it? Peak performance. Who the heck are peak performers, after all? Olympic athletes, Fortune 500 CEO's, Navy Seals. Well, yes, all of them are certainly peak performers. But please don't be intimidated by that. That's not necessarily who we're talking about here. Our definition of peak performance simply means to realize your full potential. In a very well known business magazine, there was a recent survey that asked business owners what they really wanted from their business. The answers might surprise you. "To realize my full potential" was number one and "to advance or improve" was number two. But despite brief moments of insight and genius, we humans often fall far below our real potential. Why?? Because almost nobody teaches us how to do it. So few people actually achieve their full potential that there is almost no emphasis placed on it. There's an old saying that says "we don't know what we don't know". If most people don't know how to achieve their highest levels, how can they teach it to others? So that's what we're going to be emphasizing here, simply the ability to reach your full potential as an insurance broker and as a person. We're going to get you on the road to unlocking more of that potential. We're not talking radical changes (unless you want them). We're talking about just being better than you were yesterday, making one better decision than you did yesterday. We also want you to understand that peak performance is orchestrated. It never happens by accident. What your own "full potential" is will be decided by you. Only you can really understand that. Some of the things that we'll be working on throughout the rest of the book will help you come to understand what your full potential is. You may have never really given it much thought. We know we hadn't before we started researching this material. It's easy to let life sort of just happen to us every day, like we're some sort of bystander with not much control over the situation. That was our first key in understanding peak performance, the idea that we and only we can understand our true potential and are the only ones responsible for making it happen. Taking proactive responsibility was such a refreshing change vs. drifting along and whining about it.

But seriously, why on earth should you care about peak performance? It sounds kind of new agey and you're pretty busy running your practice or agency. Well, as it turns out, there are a bunch of reasons to care. First and foremost, the bottom line is the bottom line. It's a small percentage of brokers that make real, long term money in the quantities that they really want. Most fall far short of what their real financial dreams are. Being a peak performer gives you a clear competitive advantage over mediocre performers. We know that sounds completely obvious. But if it's so obvious, why are so many people ok with being mediocre performers? Also, being a peak performer removes fear and anxiety. With so many of the brokers we've worked with, we've seen their performance skyrocket when they were able to remove fear and anxiety from their day to day existence. We've seen people's financial picture change drastically when fear and anxiety were removed as well. In our experience, peak performers also feel a sense of real, earned pride. It adds real value to mental health and well being when someone is performing at their best.

Unfortunately, over the years we've witnessed a few people that have shown a downright refusal to invest in their personal and professional excellence. And sadly, it almost always guarantees a future loss. Laziness and satisfaction with the status quo never lead anywhere good. They certainly don't lead to financial freedom and time freedom. Since you're taking the time to read this book, it's unlikely that you are one of the lazy ones who are waiting for magic to happen. Just make sure that mediocrity doesn't work its way into your thinking and acting.

Another aspect of human behavior that we've witnessed over and over is the real desire of most brokers to express the very best of who they are. Many people seem to have the internal drive and motivation for mastery. It's actually quite encouraging. Peak performance allows us to express our best selves. And we've also found that peak performers are better problem solvers and see more options and opportunity.

So, if that's not enough reasons to get you fired up about being a peak performer, then we're not sure what else to do. If more money, more time, more freedom, long term financial health, and well being aren't enough, perhaps you should check out a book on developing internal motivation. But we have a funny feeling that most of you possess plenty of internal motivation. We're just here to coax it out of you.

How will you know or evaluate whether or not you are operating at your full potential? As we mentioned, that will be decided by you and requires the ability and willingness to be honest with yourself. But we've also derived a set of components that we believe are part of being a peak performer. In other words, there are some components to measure against when examining whether or not you are being your best. Before you run away screaming, we need to give you fair warning that you're about to hear a word you've heard a thousand times before. It's a word you've heard so many times that it probably sounds like a platitude by now. What's even worse, chapter 3 is completely dedicated to this dreaded word. But we're going to go ahead and say it anyway...vision. There it is. We said it. Peak performance starts with a clear vision you are dedicated to. There is no way around it. It's one of those ancient truths we mentioned earlier. We won't devote any time to it here because there will be a whole chapter about it. But it is the first component. Other components are clear objectives, goals, and performance based measurements based on your vision. This brings it from the macro to the micro level in a pragmatic, useable format. Peak performance also requires a clear perception of reality. We're great at kidding ourselves and protecting our egos. But we need to have a grasp on reality to be our best. A few other components of peak performance would be continued freshness, peak experiences, strong relationships, self discipline, a strong support system, a culture of performance in your practice or agency, and continuous, massive action toward your vision. If you are experiencing all of these components, you are very likely a peak performer.

We're going to be taking a look at a number of these components as the book progresses.

As important as it is to discuss what peak performance is. It's also important to spend a few minutes on some common myths about peak performance.

Myth 1: A total effort and total performance is required all the time. – Not true – It isn't about going 100 mph all day and all night striving to be the best. As we said earlier, it's about being better than yourself.

Myth 2: You can force top performance to happen on demand. Operating at our highest levels is not something that can be turned on and off like a light switch. Instead of thinking of peak performance as an event, think of it as a way of life.

Myth 3: Only many years of training leads to peak performance. By making a few adjustments, you can be performing at a higher level than ever before. It won't take you years, we promise.

Myth 4: You have to have special mental powers to achieve peak performance. You have to have some special ability to control your mind, right? Wrong. The needed mental powers to achieve peak performance are within everyone's grasp. We'll be talking a lot about mind management.

Myth 5: You can sustain peak performance by sheer will power. Will power is a very limited commodity. We can't count on it for the long haul. But there are better ways…

Myth 6: Peak performers are born that way.   There is no doubt that we are each born with certain talents and abilities that others don't possess and vice versa. That being said, peak performance is something that is honed over time. It's a never ending process.

Myth 7: Peak performers know exactly why they are peak performers. Actually, much of the time when we're operating at peak performance, we're not analyzing every little aspect. We often find ourselves in "the zone" with no real conscious thought as to how we got there.

Myth 8: You can never be too motivated. Not true. A high level of motivation is required but we need to temper our motivation with realism. If we don't, we can sometimes make poor decisions or lose sight of the bigger picture.

Myth 9: Peak performers are perfectionists. Some may be. But it's certainly not a requirement. Peak performers come in all different walks of life with all different personality types.

Myth 10: Peak performers don't need coaching. We all need coaching. We can all benefit from someone who can help us bring out our best.

Myth 11: Peak performers never show weakness. Peak performance isn't about getting everything right. You're going to mess things up just as much as before. No need to pretend to not have any weaknesses.

Before we end this chapter, we wanted to also share a few things that we've seen over the past 10 years that can most definitely prevent us from achieving our best. We simply want you to be aware of them so you can avoid falling into some of these traps.

What prevents us from achieving peak performance?

- We don't take ownership of our roles and responsibilities.
- We don't know exactly what we want or why we're doing it.
- We tend to gravitate toward a steady state, meaning we don't like a lot of change.
- Changing habits is difficult/lazy habits/lazy thinking
- We don't understand that peak performance happens in the "doing". We think it's some "thing" we'll see in the future.

- ➢ We get stuck in the day to day routines.
- ➢ We don't take the time to train for peak performance.
- ➢ We don't celebrate the victories.
- ➢ We beat ourselves up.
- ➢ Wrong support system or no support system.
- ➢ Wrong information
- ➢ We don't know how to control our mind.
- ➢ Limiting beliefs

So, now that you know what peak performance is, what it isn't, common myths, and what prevents peak performance, it's time to move on to what we call the E Compass and the Four Performance Influencers. See you in chapter two.

CHAPTER 2 – THE E COMPASS AND THE FOUR PERFORMANCE INFLUENCERS

In our peak performance training and coaching programs, we focus on four specific topics. Our research and practice lead us to the conclusion that peak performance evolves from mastering these four particular areas that we've come to call the E Compass and the Four Performance Influencers. There are a number of subtopics under each of the four performance influencers, which we'll dive into throughout the rest of the book. But everything that we discuss falls under one of the four, which is why it's so important to introduce the concept to you here.

We probably want to define for second what e stands for in the E Compass. The E in our compass is the "ergogenic" compass. For those of you who are athletes, you may have heard this phrase before. But ergogenic simply means "intended to enhance performance, stamina, and ability". So we call it the e compass. After years of research, we broke the concept down into these four primary areas. The four primary influencers of performance are :

> ➤ **Vision**
> ➤ **Mind Management**
> ➤ **Relationship Management**

➤ **Performance Based Measurement/Goals**

If it seems overly simplistic to explain performance as they relate to these four performance influencers, we understand. Please, stick with us. It will all make sense as we go along. You'll be amazed at how almost every aspect of your performance is influenced by one of these four items. Besides, who needs something that's way too complicated? We'd far rather provide you with useful stuff that you can apply, not a bunch of fancy nonsense.

We found that if one can master or at least be highly proficient in these areas they can greatly improve their performance. We can hear your mind already. It's screaming at you saying, "What in the world do these have to do with growing my insurance practice?"! Read on, you'll see.

The four performance influencers are going to provide you with a solid foundation and roadmap from which you can take your career in whatever direction you choose. You'll examine each aspect of performance in a way you never have before and you'll see how they blend together in a way that will cause you to be a better broker than before you started this book. For example, we suspect that you've been told about the importance of vision many times throughout your career. But...how clear and specific are you at this moment about where your practice is going, why it's going there, and how it's getting there? We'd venture to guess that it's probably not as clear as you might think. When is the last time you sat down and created a precise plan for your life and business? Probably not recently. But without a clear and compelling vision, elite performance simply doesn't happen. When is the last time you clearly outlined your strengths and planned the majority of your activities around those strengths? Probably never. But you can't imagine how much utilizing your strengths improves your performance.

In the chapters that are based on **mind management**, you'll discover how working on your talent, skills, and confidence will propel you. You'll understand which of your talents and skills are helping your practice and you'll know what skills you need to acquire to perform at the level you want. You'll learn how your ego messes with you and hinders your progress and what to do about it. You'll also be a better **critical thinker** than you were before and see how it is vital in growing your practice.

You'll know from the **relationship management** chapters how managing the relationships with yourself and others can be the most important factor in growing your practice and being an elite performer. And you'll have a system for tracking and monitoring your progress.

See...we told you that the four performance influencers have a lot to do with being a high performance broker. We'll go into plenty of detail as we go along and leave no stones unturned. Wow, that sounded profound.

You'll find that virtually everything you do and every behavior you engage in can be improved by mastering the four performance influencers. It's been an amazing thing to watch other brokers' practices grow by leaps and bounds after they put them into practice. And we're certain the same thing can happen for you.

So strap on your seatbelt. We're about to talk about vision in a way that you've never looked at it before. We want you to spend as much time as necessary on the next chapter. This is really, really, really important. This will be the keystone of your performance. It will be what helps you persevere through the challenging times. It will be what provides the internal motivation you need to perform at your best. Take this seriously. Your vision is the reason you do what you do.

CHAPTER 3 – VISION AND WHY YOU NEED ONE

We'd like you to meet Mr. X (likely not his real name). Mr. X has been a broker for more than 20 years, and a rather successful one at that. He was making decent money, had a staff of one, and was working way too many hours. He was fairly happy but not ecstatic. He was looking for more balance in his life, while at the same time trying to figure out how to grow his practice, as he had been rather stagnant for a few years. Things weren't bad by any stretch. They were just flat. And frankly, Mr. X was feeling a little flat too. He said he had always been really good at the sales aspect, so that wasn't the problem. He knows how to sell. And he really enjoys being in the business. So what was the problem?

Mr. X started working with us about 3 years ago. The first place we started with was "well, what do you really want"? Guess what...he hadn't really thought about it that much. He was so busy just running has practice and his life that he hadn't really given much thought to exactly what he wished were different, what he wanted instead, and how to achieve it. That was an eye opening moment for him.

Another broker we work with had been part of another agency for several years. He kept saying to himself "I know I've got a better way". The broker he worked for wasn't hearing any of it. He wanted things as they were. After all, they were working just fine. Why change? But our friend just couldn't get it out of his system. He had an idea of exactly how he would run an agency, what product lines he wanted to carry, and the types of clients he wanted to work with. He finally left and started his own agency. Although it hasn't been completely easy, he is much happier and is taking his agency exactly the direction he wanted to. And it's working.

Another client, Sarah, has also been a broker for many years, at least 10. Just like Mr. X, things were "fine" but there were a few things nagging at her. She knew she wanted to grow her practice but also wanted to spend more time with her children and find a little more time for herself. A daunting task, right? And again like Mr. X, she never gave much solid thought as to how to make all of that happen. It was almost like an out of reach fantasy that would be nice "someday". Do you have any of those? All of those things you'll accomplish someday? The life that you'd really like to live but you're way too busy right now? We've seen people fall into this trap over and over. Often times the biggest problem is that we haven't created a clear idea of what we really want. We drift along wherever the current takes, wherever life takes us. We don't realize that simply by deciding, in clear detail, what we really want, things no longer need to be a "someday" dream. The first step to being a high performance broker is deciding exactly what it is you want. Chances are, you haven't taken the time to do this in a very long time, if ever.

Vision isn't that boring statement you wrote near the top of your business plan. It's the reason you do what you do. It's what compels you, motivates you, makes you work through the challenges. Vision is that thing that you want more than anything. A strong vision alone can dramatically increase your business and personal performance.

What is vision and why is it relevant to peak performance?

Knowing where you're going and why you're engaged in specific behaviors requires having a clear vision. A vision builds trust, collaboration, interdependence, motivation, and mutual responsibility for success. Vision helps people make smart choices because their decisions are being made with the end result in mind. As goals are accomplished, the answer to "What is next?" becomes clear. Vision allows people to act from a proactive stance, moving toward what they want rather than reactively away from what they don't want. Pursuing a vision also fulfills us personally and emotionally. Peak performance is not possible if we're not working toward something meaningful and compelling.

Why is it so important for a business leader to have vision?

Because leadership is about going somewhere. If you don't know where you're going, what does your leadership matter? Vision isn't some "pie in the sky" concept that it would be nice to pursue some day. It's your reason for existence. What's yours?

There's something important you need to understand about vision that we believe confuses a lot of people. We attended a seminar a year or so ago and the presenter was asking people what their vision was. One person stated that they wanted to win the Nobel Prize. Now, we're not here to judge whether or not that person was qualified to win the Nobel Prize or had an idea that was Nobel Prize worthy. It became clear pretty quickly, however, that the person that said it didn't believe it at all. There are two very important points to remember about vision. First, it doesn't need to be grandiose. Your vision doesn't have to be some grand plan to change the world. It seems that many people have been told that you need to create some grand, huge, change the world, type of vision. That's not at all what we're talking about. If you want to pursue a world changing vision, please do so.

We are certainly not here to squash anybody's dream. But what we mean by vision is "what would your life and business look like if they were exactly as you wanted them to be"? What is going to provide you with the happiest most fulfilling life? Your vision is what will bring the most meaning and purpose to your life. It can be something simple as long as it provides you with the internal motivation to pursue it. How will you change your little piece of the world? Second, you have to believe it. If you don't believe it's true or possible, you're kind of wasting your time. Simple and believable are two great places to start.

Oh, and one more thing about vision...we can't tell you how many times we've heard someone say "my vision is to make more money". There are so many reasons why that's a crappy vision. But we'll give you a few specific ones. First, we've never seen it work. If someone is just chasing a dollar, we usually see them end up with none. It's also not a very compelling vision. It's not something that will keep you motivated and excited to get to work. It will very quickly become a burden. Also, from our own experience and the experiences of our clients, when someone is pursuing a vision that really means something to them, the money seems to flow much better. Yes, we all need money and want more of it but it's not really a vision. Needing more money is always a fear based vision. We want you to create something that motivates and excites you.

Some find that their vision isn't really career related. There may be something other than work that really moves you that your career can help you support.

Example: We had a client who held a passion for missionary work. But found that in order to support that passion and his family he needed to work. His compromise was to work a business with flexible hours, put aside a portion of his earnings, and plan shorter missionary trips. This allowed him to have the best of both world;, raise a family and do missionary work.

We also completely realize that things change over time. What your business looks like today might be something totally different in 5 years. That's perfectly fine. As we learn more, discover more, hear new ideas, etc., we may decide to change our plans or direction. We get that. That being said, having some clear focus to guide your behaviors, efforts, and thoughts will put you ahead of 95% of the pack. The "seat of the pants" operation of our business or life may somewhat work but it will never allow you to be a peak performer or a top earner. Vision will help you make your day to day decisions in a more productive way and help you to stay motivated during the challenging times.

We hope we've convinced you that the first step in becoming a high performance agent is a clear and compelling vision. To help you along, we've created an extensive vision exercise, one like you've never seen before. Take the time to carefully go through the whole exercise. Yes, it's going to take a little while. There's not much we could do about that. You might also find that you end up answering question #1 last. That's ok too. Do this exercise in a way that works for you and we'll see you on the other side.

A Comprehensive Vision Exercise

In order to gain access to your full potential, you first need a compelling reason to push your own limits. Our research and work with insurance agents has shown that to prosper at the level that one wants, the practice needs to operate through conscious design, not by chance or accident.

We have devised an exercise that will help you identify your own vision. You may already be clear on what your vision is. You may not. Either way, go through the exercise and we think you'll learn a lot about yourself and be left with a stronger, more compelling vision and direction.

Before we go further, I'd like to explain that there are two types of motivation, extrinsic and intrinsic. Extrinsic factors are those that come from outside of ourselves and motivate us to take action, i.e., to avoid punishment, to gain favor, to earn reward, etc. The other form of motivation is intrinsic. These are factors that come from within ourselves that are a source of motivation. For this exercise, we will be focused on intrinsic motivators. These are what really drive our performance.

Conventional decisions are almost always extrinsically motivated and fear based. Creating a vision takes courage. We need to be willing to be as courageous as possible when discovering our vision and making decisions. Figuring out why we do what we do is difficult and sometimes inaccurate. This exercise will provide a sense of clarity of your goals and direction.

Need help with this?

We have some completed examples to act as your guide. Go to

http://mentalcompass.com/your-practice/

and they will be sent right to you by email.

Let's get started...

1. **What would an insurance practice look like that creates a good life for you?**
    ⇒ What types of insurance?
    ⇒ Where would you be located?
    ⇒ What hours would you work?
    ⇒ What types of people would you work with?
    ⇒ What kinds of customers would you work with?
    ⇒ Would you have employees?
    ⇒ What types of employees would you have? What would they be like?
    ⇒ How far would your commute be?
    ⇒ How much family time would it allow for you?
    ⇒ How much revenue would it generate?
    ⇒ How much profit would it generate?

This is big picture time. We want you to start thinking about exactly what your practice would look like (i.e. your vision) in order for it to provide you exactly the life you want.

2. It would be better if…What is that "better" in your industry or practice?

3. What makes me really mad? (circumstances, products, something missing, situations) Be creative here. What truly frustrates you that needs to change in your business/life/industry/world?

4. What type of "project(s)" would you like to be involved with? How do you think you are most capable/best suited to create your ideal situation?

5. Do a brain dump and sort out the details;
   ⇒ What types of products/solutions/projects could YOU create that will achieve your ideal scenario?
   ⇒ What types of people do you need to be surrounded with?
   ⇒ What type of environment do you need to be in?
   ⇒ What else needs to happen in your life as you pursue this? What are your other existing responsibilities?

⇒ Are there additional ways I can generate revenue?

⇒ Do they fit in with what I am currently doing?

⇒ What roles and responsibilities do you want in this project?

⇒ How do you need to be mentally and physically to pursue this?

⇒ What head trash is in the way of pursuing your vision?

6. Ask yourself, "am I willing to be accountable for this"? Be candid here. Be specific about what you are actually willing to do and what you're not.

7. Ask yourself, "what personal needs of mine will be fulfilled by pursuing my vision"?

8. What else do I need to achieve this?

9. Which of my signature strengths will be most called upon to achieve this?

10. What skills am I currently lacking that are needed to achieve this? Am I willing to learn them?

11. Am I willing to take the time, energy, focused attention, and persistence to see this through?

12. Is the message clear to you?

13. What has held you back from pursuing your vision? Or, what might possibly hold you back in the future?

We don't expect that this exercise will be complete your first time through. You might come back to it over and over in the coming months to tweak it or add to it as you think of new things. That's ok. It wasn't meant to be done in a day, especially if you haven't really thought about this concept much before now.

We ask you to go through the rest of this book with a purpose driven mindset. It is the first step in unlocking your full potential.

In the next chapter, we're going to get into your signature strengths and why they are important to becoming a high performance insurance broker. Stick with us!

Chapter 4 – Your Signature Strengths and Why They Matter

We have a client that we've worked with for several years (can't seem to think of a creative name for him at the moment, so we'll just call him "that guy"). When we first met that guy, life and business seemed to be a continuous struggle. He was doing ok at best, sometimes far less than ok. He's a bright enough fellow, probably way above average intelligence. But he had become a chronic underachiever who was rather disillusioned much of the time. This bothered him more than you can imagine, especially because he didn't know what was wrong. Why was he watching several of his colleagues have great success while he was usually wondering why he hadn't become a crab fisherman instead of an insurance broker? As you can imagine, he wasn't happy much of the time and everything work related was a grind. He was an avid reader of self help books and attended lots of seminars. Still nothing changed. We met him when he was rapidly approaching the end of his rope in the business.

We discovered quickly that he had developed some pretty strong beliefs over the years about what kind of person an insurance broker was and what they weren't. According to that guy, good brokers were all type A, hard charging, master sales people who wanted to do nothing but work. Sure, they cared deeply about their clients but if you're not out hustling, you're falling behind. You have to hand out your business card to everyone who is within 10 feet and always be closing. Sounds pretty darn exhausting, doesn't it? Also, none of those ideas he held in his head were him at all. He's actually a very laid back guy who really wants to run a great practice and have real balance in his life. Even worse, none of those things he would use to describe a successful broker matched his strengths in any way, shape, or form. What do we mean by his strengths? What are we referring to? Read on. Now it gets really exciting. You're going to learn about your signature strengths.

We are going to dig deep into a concept that is probably going to be pretty new to you. We're going to talk to you about your signature strengths and how you can use them to be a high performance broker. This can be a little bit confusing for some people. But please bear with us. We'll make it as clear as possible.

One of the things we've seen some struggle with from time to time is that feeling that they should be a certain way. "If I were a great _____, I'd be type A, persistent, self regulated and funny". We've seen people come up with all sorts of labels of what they should and shouldn't be like. What they don't realize is that they would be far better off discovering and utilizing their strengths, rather than trying to fix perceived weaknesses.

A ton of research, especially in the field of positive psychology, has shown that people are more successful and happier when they utilize their signature strengths.

> They're financially better off
> More productive
> Less stressed
> Less tired
> And definitely more energized.

Let's make sure we clarify one thing here. Let's make sure we distinguish between strengths and talents. The way we like to describe it is, your strengths are who you are. Your talents are what you can do. We will discuss talents in the next chapter.

Your signature strengths are those strengths that best describe the positive aspects of who you are. When you are using them they make you feel engaged, energized, and comfortable. Your family and friends would immediately agree that when you are exercising your strengths you come across as your best. Finding ways to use and express these strengths is going to bring you the most benefit.

Your signature strengths are kind of your fall back default position. We are going to emphasize a lot in this chapter that to be your best, the idea is to use your signature strengths, not try to fix your lesser strengths.

Yes, we said lesser strengths not weakness. We will talk more about that later.

According to Dr. Martin Seligman, your signature strengths are those strengths that best describe the positive aspects of who you are. These strengths are strong capacities in you and they are probably engaging, energizing, and comfortable for you to use. Your family and friends would immediately agree these are important strengths that you have. Finding ways to use and express these strengths is likely to bring you many benefits, and can help you create your best life, personally and professionally.

Utilizing our signature strengths helps us to thrive. Our signature strengths are our valued styles of thinking, feeling, and acting that contribute to a fulfilling life and a successful business. Research on the value of utilizing our signature strengths has become a major focus in recent years, with an explosion of information that discusses identifying and using strengths in your business or in your personal life. When we focus on our signature strengths, we have a tendency to accomplish goals more effectively and are "stuck" far less often.

When we focus on our strengths, it enhances our odds of achieving peak performance. Research has shown that when we worry less about our weaknesses and focus more on our strengths, we thrive.

We're going to provide you a little background here. A lot of our research has come from studying Positive Psychology. Drs. Martin Seligman and Chris Peterson are the founders of this science. Prior to Positive Psychology, the science of Psychology was focused on fixing what was wrong with us.   Dr. Martin Seligman wondered what would happen if we focused on what was right about us. He felt that people would be better off in the long run if the focus was on developing, utilizing, and exploiting our strengths, rather than trying to fix our perceived weaknesses. He discovered that people truly thrive when they focus more on their strengths. The VIA strengths assessment is a by-product of this research. The 24 strengths that are represented in this assessment are strengths that we were all born with the ability to perform. They aren't things that had to be learned. Throughout our lifetime we unconsciously prioritized these strengths.

The VIA Survey of Character Strengths Measures 24 Character Strengths, and helps you identify what is strongest in you. The top 5 of your character strengths are known as your signature strengths. These are the strengths that will help you achieve the greatest results. We'd like you to stop reading for a few minutes and go take the assessment. This information is crucial to becoming a peak performer.

Go take the assessment at www.viacharacter.org, and then we can move on. You will have the option to take this assessment for free, or purchase the full report. The free report will simply provide you with prioritization of your strengths. The purchased report will offer additional information that could help you better understand the report. Either way, we strongly recommend you take the assessment so you can have this information at your fingertips.

Instructions on taking the VIA Strengths Assessment:

1. *www.viame.org/survey/Surveys/TakeSurvey*
2. *Login Username create username*
3. *Select I want to take the VIA Survey of Character (VIA-IS)*
4. *Click Begin Survey*
5. *Complete survey*
6. *On the "Survey Completed" screen, under Option 1, click "View Rankings Here" to see your results.*

7. ****Important for free report** *click show all results, copy and paste into a word document; make sure all 24 strengths are included.*

We're not naïve. We know there will be one or two of you who don't go and take the assessment. It would be such a shame though. So just go ahead and do it. Otherwise we're just going to nag you until you do and it's going to become really annoying. So just go get it over with. You'll be glad you did.

Since you've likely taken the assessment by now, let's talk in a little more detail about signature strengths

The work of positive psychologists like Martin Seligman appears to show that the happiest and most successful people are those that have discovered their unique strengths and utilize them as often as possible.

You may have had certain strengths that are so natural to you that you may not even consider them strengths. Think about an episode in your life when you were at your very best. What qualities enabled you to perform like that? When Drs. Martin Seligman and Chris Peterson sought to discover and

39

classify commonly held strengths and virtues across cultures, they created a classification of core virtues that humans morally value no matter their cultural, racial, and religious differences.

Current research indicates that you are most likely to value a job, relationship, hobby or institution that aligns with your core signature strengths and allows you to regularly utilize them. In fact, research indicates that one of the best ways to boost your long-term happiness is to use your strengths in new ways and situations, rather than focusing on your weaknesses. This is well in keeping with the philosophy of positive psychology. We mentioned at the beginning that this was not a book about positive thinking. And positive psychology and positive thinking are quite different concepts. But the basic idea behind positive psychology is the focus on strengths and well being. When we spend our efforts on our strengths, we find ourselves in a state of well being far more often.

When Dr. Martin Seligman came up with the concept of assessing strengths, he called the top 5 your signature strengths. Out of the 24 identified strengths, your lower ones he refers to as your lesser strengths.

This is so important we're going to say it again

Lesser strengths do not represent weaknesses but instead simply indicate that there are other strengths more strongly represented. These are strengths that are expressed less often and/or less comfortably.

By the way there aren't any good or bad strengths, they are just strengths. Some folks will look at their report and immediately feel disappointed that they don't have certain strengths in a higher position, or that certain strengths that they deem frivolous or silly are located in the top positions. As we mentioned earlier, this chapter is about utilizing your top strengths, not wishing they were different. Peak Performance is achieved by utilizing what is best about us, not wishing we were something else.

We have seen hundreds of these assessments and have never seen 2 with identical results. Each report is truly unique to the individual.

So how does this help you?

We have seen that when you utilize your top strengths

➢ You are more likely to spend time on the activities and get the results you desire
➢ You feel more confident which leads to feeling more competent

Look at your report. Are your top strengths an accurate picture of you? Remember, there aren't any weaknesses. And, don't be alarmed if honesty falls low on your list. This doesn't make you a dishonest person.

Go through your results. When looking at your number 1 – 5 write down how you use them in your everyday life. Your work, school, play, and family. We promise you will find it everywhere. It may take a little brain power. And don't worry, you won't think of everything right now. But make a promise to yourself to start to notice where these strengths show up. We have been noticing for 3 years now, and still keep discovering more about our strengths.

Middle strengths???

We spend a lot of time talking about your top strengths and your lesser strengths, but what about the strengths 6-19? We don't want to sound dismissive and say that they aren't important, but we have also found that they don't play as big a role as the top and bottom strengths. They are just in the middle. If you want to spend some time thinking about them, then notice where they fall on your list. The ones closer to the top will feel better and easier to use, the ones closer to the bottom won't. If you purchased the report, you will notice that each strength has a score next to it, sometimes the scoring is so tight that your top strengths can reach beyond the top 5. Once again, don't worry so much about them.

This is important to mention: If you see a strength on your report that isn't one of your top 5 that you feel is a top strength, use it, the goal is to help you understand what is best about you. Don't get mired down by details. Essentially, If creativity is your 8th strength and you enjoy creative work, keep being creative.

This can be overwhelming if you try to find all the answers at once. We have found that committing to noticing how you use your strengths is the best way to learn. Be deliberate about it, every day just start to notice where you are using your top strengths and how you feel when you use them. Also, pay attention to when your lesser strengths are being called upon, and how you feel when you are using those.

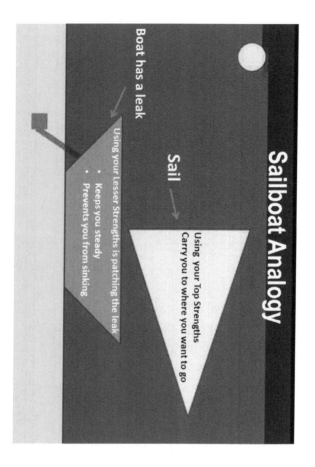

There are some strengths that people ask about often. We can't go through a detailed explanation of every strength here, but we would like to highlight the ones commonly asked about.

What if creativity is your top strength? Creativity can mean a number of things but if we want to strip it down, it means making something from nothing, finding a solution, or putting things together. You may not be an artist per se. You are simply someone who can see beyond what exists in front of you. If a friend or co-worker has a problem, you have the ability to tear it apart, make sense of it, and find solutions. Maybe you create a certain recipe that just pops into your head. Maybe you see recipes just as a basic guide that you should experiment with anyway. But you definitely have a knack for creating something where it didn't exists before.

As important as your strengths are, we also want to be cautious and aware of where our strengths may not work for us. Continuing with the example of creativity, as valuable as creativity may be for a business owner, it may not always be called for. An obvious area where you may want to temper your creativity would be your financials. Creative books make for visits from the IRS. In business, it's also important to have process and procedure. You can't always just change the way you do things on a whim. It will create chaos and your employees won't like it.

It becomes very tempting to spice things up with a little change. This can lead to stagnancy. Why?

The job never gets finished. If you are in business clients and employees may not get as excited about the constant changes. They will also get confused and disgruntled if they never know what the day is going to be like. Finally, creative people like to offer suggestions to others on how it can be better. Unless someone asks, assume they don't want your help.

Some of you may have spirituality as your top strength. Many business owners are confused as to how spirituality can be a business strength. According to Dr. Seligman, the creator of the VIA assessment, he doesn't necessarily mean someone who is devoted to a religion. He means more someone who is committed to a religious organization. So what does a religious organization ask of you? It asks that you are part of a community, follow a certain philosophy, and look out for your fellow man/woman. Spirituality also asks you to think of yourself as part of a bigger society, purpose, or world, something bigger than yourself? Can't you see how some of those qualities could help you run a successful business? This can be a great strength to possess when you're building a team.

Just like creativity (or any of the other strengths, for that matter), there are times when you may want to temper your use of spirituality. You want to be cautious about pushing your beliefs on others (religious or otherwise). If they aren't asking, they may not want to know.

Kindness is another that is hard for business professionals to wrap their heads around. How can you lead with kindness, or how does this apply? Once again, strip it down. What is kindness? How are you currently using it? We find the best way to figure out a solution is to look at your history. Especially the history of your successes. Think of a time when you have used this strength, and break it down. Perhaps you are remembering an experience when you anonymously gave a gift, or paid someone's toll fee. What are the details? This seems like a lot of work, and at first a bit strange, but over time you will start to see a pattern and make sense of it. Don't complicate it or over think it. You've heard the saying "the devil's in the details", well, it usually is. The answer is staring at you.

Kindness may not work when it is overused. Overuse of kindness can come off as insincere. Moreover, kindness may work against us when we do things for others that we did not want to do but did anyway out of a sense of obligation. All we're saying is, as powerful as strengths are, temper their overuse. Be aware of where they best apply.

So, how do strengths work? What happens along the pathway between using our strengths and achieving success and happiness? Why are we likely to become happier when we use our signature strengths in new and unique ways?

New research published by Alex Linley and his colleagues (Linley et al., 2010) helps us answer some of these questions. In the first study to explore the connections between strengths use, goal progress, psychological needs, and well-being, the researchers found that those who used their signature strengths ultimately:

- ➢ Made more progress on their goals
- ➢ Met their basic psychological needs (autonomy, relatedness, and competence)
- ➢ Were higher in overall well-being (a combination of higher life satisfaction, higher positive emotions, and lower negative emotions)

This makes good, practical sense. Signature strengths come naturally to us; they are an expression of who we are. Therefore, when we allow that core part of ourselves to be expressed, we are meeting basic human needs that have to do with making connections in our relationships and accomplishing as much as we can in this life.

Success with our goals naturally flows from this. As a result, we experience greater happiness.

How can you use these findings in your practice? There appears to be a natural progression of steps you can follow:

➢ Take the VIA Survey to determine your rank order of character strengths from 1 to 24.
➢ Discern which strengths are your true "signature" (ranked in your top 5).
➢ Explore these strengths deeply (e.g., past use, current use, application to a future best self, use at the most difficult times, use at the times when you were strongest).
➢ Set goals that align with your personal values and strengths.
➢ Find new and unique ways to apply your signature strengths to your goals.

Distinction: Like everything, there is a Yin and Yang to strengths use as well. Whether we realize it or not, we are always striving to use our top strengths. However, there are times when strengths are either over used, or underused. The best way to figure out how you are using the strength is to analyze how you feel when you are using it.

For example: Forgiveness is best used when you are truly forgiving someone for something they have done to you. Overuse could be forgiveness when you weren't sincere about it. Underuse could be beating yourself up and not forgiving yourself.

Ok, for the one of you that is not going to actually go and take the strengths assessment, here are the 24 character strengths (not in any particular order). At the very least, go through these with someone you trust very much and try to figure out your top 5.

Creativity (originality, ingenuity): Thinking of novel and productive ways to conceptualize and do things.

Curiosity (interest, novelty-seeking, openness to experience): Taking an interest in ongoing experiences for its own sake; exploring and discovering.

Open-mindedness (judgment, critical thinking): Thinking things through and examining them from all sides; weighing all evidence fairly.

Love of learning: Mastering new skills, topics, and bodies of knowledge, whether on one's own or formally.

Perspective (wisdom): Being able to provide wise counsel to others; having ways of looking at the world that make sense to oneself and to other people.

Bravery (valor): Not shrinking from threat, challenge, difficulty, or pain; acting on convictions even if unpopular.

Persistence (perseverance, industriousness): Finishing what one starts; persisting in a course of action in spite of obstacles.

Integrity (authenticity, honesty): Presenting oneself in a genuine way; taking responsibility for one's feeling and actions.

Vitality (zest, enthusiasm, vigor, energy): Approaching life with excitement and energy; feeling alive and activated.

Love: Valuing close relations with others, in particular those in which sharing and caring are reciprocated.

Kindness (generosity, nurturance, care, compassion, altruistic love, "niceness"): Doing favors and good deeds for others.

Social intelligence (emotional intelligence, personal intelligence): Being aware of the motives and feelings of other people and oneself.

Citizenship (social responsibility, loyalty, teamwork): Working well as a member of a group or team; being loyal to the group.

Fairness: Treating all people the same according to notions of fairness and justice; not letting personal feelings bias decisions about others.

Leadership: Excelling at the tasks of leadership: encouraging a group to get things done and preserving harmony within the group by making everyone feel included. Excels at organizing activities and seeing that they happen.

Forgiveness and mercy: Forgiving those who have done wrong; accepting the shortcomings of others; giving people a second chance; not being vengeful.

Humility / Modesty: Letting one's accomplishments speak for themselves; not regarding oneself as more special than one is.

Prudence: Being careful about one's choices; not taking undue risks; not saying or doing things that might later be regretted.

Self-regulation (self-control): Regulating what one feels and does; being disciplined; controlling one's appetites and emotions.

Appreciation of beauty and excellence (awe, wonder, elevation): Appreciating beauty, excellence, and/or skilled performance in various domains of life.

Gratitude: Being aware of and thankful of the good things that happen; taking time to express thanks.

Hope (optimism, future-mindedness, future orientation): Expecting the best in the future and working to achieve it.

Humor (playfulness): Liking to laugh and tease; bringing smiles to other people; seeing the light side.

Spirituality (religiousness, faith, purpose): Having coherent beliefs about the higher purpose, the meaning of life, and the meaning of the universe.

This description of the signature strengths comes directly from the VIA Character Assessment. www.viacharacter.org

We understand that there was a lot to try to absorb in this chapter. Please don't feel overwhelmed. Go back through it a few times if you need to.

The bottom line about character strengths is this...when you spend much more time focusing on using and exploiting your strengths, you have a seriously higher chance of reaching your goals than when you focus on trying to fix your lesser strengths. It's that simple. Find a way to incorporate your strengths into your insurance practice every day. If you don't, you're going to feel just like "that guy". Make sense?

Now, not to be confused with signature strengths are your talents and skills. So in the next chapter, we're going to discuss talent, skill, and self confidence. It's the next step in your journey.

CHAPTER 5 – TALENT, SKILL, AND SELF CONFIDENCE

Not to be confused with strengths, let's spend some time on talent, skill, and self confidence. We've been asked a bunch of times what the difference between strengths and talents are. Consider your strengths as who you are. Consider your talents as what you can do. A subtle but distinct difference.

This isn't a chapter we need to spend a ton of time and words on but there are some crucial distinctions that will make your understanding of peak performance and your pursuit of it all the more fruitful. But for this chapter to have the greatest impact, you need to be honest with yourself and be willing to take an honest assessment of your talents. It's time to check the ego at the door. By the way, we'll talk a lot more about ego protection a little later.

We have another client, Pat, who was always on top of his game. He had a successful practice, was active in the community, two kids, and was full of confidence...almost to a point of being cocky. Then one day his wife told him she was done and was divorcing him. Right around that time, he was having issues with his administrative assistant. Oh, and on top of it, a new website he had created to go along with a new offering turned out to not create any results whatsoever. Zero.

You can likely imagine what happened. Over time, his practice got slower. He became a bit despondent but tried to hide it with fake laughs and big stories. Then, a few months later, people heard from him less and less. What had happened to him? In a nutshell, his confidence was shattered.

We know a married couple that also happen to be business partners. OK, it's us. In 2004, we had a former business partner steal $89,000 from the business, which was pretty much everything we had at the time. The police wouldn't touch it, calling it a civil matter. That's a story for another day. But the loss of that money was a huge blow. Other aspects of our business suffered. We suffered financially. Our relationship suffered. It almost felt like we couldn't do anything right for a very long time. Once again, shattered confidence.

The loss of confidence can be debilitating. You've seen it before. When someone loses their confidence, they become an entirely different person. A shell of their former self.

Several months ago, we had a conversation with one of the all time great women's basketball players, Jennifer Rizzotti. You probably remember her if you're a basketball fan. She was a star at the University of Connecticut, where she helped them win national championships. She also played in the WNBA. Now, she's the head coach at the University of Hartford. She had a lot of fascinating things to say about confidence and performance. She said that, in her opinion, self confidence was the single biggest factor in peak performance. The belief in yourself and your capabilities is paramount to performance. She went on to say that, the ones with the most self confidence also seemed to practice the most and work on their skills the most. It was like climbing a ladder. The more they utilized their talents and skills, the more they were willing to practice, the more self confidence they develop. It keeps building upon itself. As we mentioned early on in the book, belief in your vision and ability to accomplish that vision are an inescapable truth about peak performance. It's required if you truly want to be at the top of your game.

Is there an inborn presence of biological or psychological attributes that we can refer to as "innate talent"? Well...there's a great deal of debate as to whether or not innate talent exists. But for the purposes of this conversation, we'd like to say, "Who cares"? Wherever they came from, we all have talents. Not to be confused with character strengths, talents are those specific aptitudes that come naturally to you.

Many performance programs will tell you, "You can do anything you set your mind to." " Find that big, audacious goal and go after it". That may or may not be true. But it's unlikely. Even if you could do anything you wanted, you probably shouldn't. We know that goes against everything you've heard before. But it's something important we've observed for many years. Peak performers are astute at discovering their talents, practicing them relentlessly until they develop into skills, and building self confidence.

Recent research has shown that **people who were using their natural talents every day were "six times more likely to be engaged in their jobs and more than three times as likely to report having an excellent quality of life."**

The single most important phrase in peak performance is **self confidence**, as you heard from Coach Rizzotti. A strong level of REAL self confidence is a strong predictor of success.

Although many talents may not apply to the pursuit of your particular vision, what is important is to find out specifically what your talents are and how you may apply the right ones to your business.

As we mentioned, consider talent, practice, and self confidence to be a ladder that continually builds on itself. As one uses their talents, they are more prone to practice and more prone to develop new skills. As we practice and develop new skills, our level of confidence continues to rise. As we feel more confidence, we are more apt to build upon the existing talent. It's a never ending cycle.

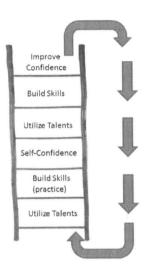

What are your talents?

Understanding your natural talents is not a difficult process. Like many of the other things we're discussing in this book, it begins with a close look at yourself.

- ➤ Reflect back over your life
- ➤ Identify those moments where things felt effortless
- ➤ What activities do you engage in where you know that you've "got it", where you feel like an expert?
- ➤ What things have people always told you that you were great at?
- ➤ What activities cause you to get into "flow"
- ➤ What activities bring you the most satisfaction?
- ➤ What activities do you like to practice the most?
- ➤ What activities do you truly look forward to in your business or life?

The biggest point we want you to take away from the last two chapters is that, instead of engaging in activities that don't utilize your strengths and talents, spend the necessary time and effort to figure out what your signature strengths and innate talents are. Then practice them and nurture them relentlessly until you feel a very high level of self confidence. That will put you ahead of 90% of your competitors.

So just to recap and not leave any confusion, let's make sure we're all clear on what we're talking about. Talent is a natural ability or aptitude. Skill is ability that stems from your knowledge, practice, and talent to do something very well. The highest performers always engage in behaviors that use their strengths and talents that lead them to have an enormous amount of skill.

In the next chapter...when you manage your mind, you manage your destiny.

Chapter 6 – Mind Management and Critical Thinking

You may have asked yourself this question many times. "Why do people see the world and circumstances so differently?" You have those friends or family members who are always gloomy, to whom the world is always doing wrong to. You might have colleagues who always see the worst in everything. Everything is always happening to them. Then there are those who seem to have an overall positive view of the world, their industry, and their life. They acknowledge that there are challenges but don't have a tendency to see them as insurmountable.

The big difference is that one has effectively figured out how to manage their mind and one has not.

When you manage your mind, you manage your destiny.

We realize that this phrase might sound a little bit hokey. But in our humble opinion, it's true. More goes on between our ears that gets in our way than any external forces ever do. When we can manage our mind, our thoughts, and our emotions, we can face our practices in a logical, non-dramatic sort of way that allows us to make better decisions and handle crises effectively. Managing our mind affectively helps us to make "moving forward", proactive decisions, rather than fear based, reactive ones. Managing our mind well provides us a more realistic world view.

Peak performance are those moments when everything comes together for an insurance broker, where things just seem to flow. The reason you are reading this book is probably to:

➢ Reach a new level or "peak" in your performance
➢ Learn in such a way as to increase the occurrence of your peak performances
➢ Learn how to consistently act at your optimal level

The main purpose for developing mental training is to understand that "mind and body cannot be separated". The state that our mind is in absolutely affects our behaviors and outcomes.

Here's perhaps the most important thing we'd like you to take away from this chapter; your thoughts about what is going on is your only experience. Let us explain...what you THINK about something is the only reality you will ever know. What you THINK about it will be the only experience you will have around it. What you THINK about something will cause the emotions you feel around it. You are either liking something or you're not. People live up to our expectations or they don't.

Circumstances are what they are. They have no inherent value. It's not reality that shapes you, it's the lens through which you view the world that shapes your reality. Now you might be thinking, oh that's not true. There are plenty of "real" things to be unhappy about. It's not my thinking. It's what's true. But guess what. Reality is what it is. That's it. What is awful to one person might be wonderful to another. We each look at certain circumstances, experiences, activities, and people with a completely different point of view. Sometimes even when people die, some people are sad about it and some could be happy. Reality is reality. Studies show that the outside world will only predict 10% of your happiness. 90% is the way that your brain processes the world. You can change your formula. But here's what we do instead;

- ➤ We name everything and start telling stories about it.
- ➤ Then we believe our stories are reality and this is the world.
- ➤ We tell stories about good, bad, right, and wrong, fair and unfair.
- ➤ We talk about how things should or shouldn't be.
- ➤ Then we compare this or that to each other.

➢ We believe this is the world...or is it just our stories?

This leads us to a topic that is difficult for many people to internalize. They intellectually understand and can see it in other people but not in themselves. So we ask you to go into this with a very open mind.

In learning to better manage your mind, we first have to share some disturbing news about your brain. That pesky brain of yours is not making life any easier.
Freud once said "our ego rejects the unbearable idea".

It is true that failure is the enemy of the ego. This is the main reason that most people don't reach peak performance or even attempt to. They don't want to risk the ego crushing blow of failure. Therefore, we engage in behaviors and activities that we think are "safe" or even worse, sometimes we're just paralyzed into taking no action whatsoever.

We could do an entire program and write 5 books on belief systems and how we're wired. This is why we say this is the most important aspect of peak performance, being better able to manage a mind that has no desire to be managed. And without an effectively managed mind, one is never able to take total control of their destiny.

We're sure you've all heard about belief systems before. We're discussing conscious beliefs. But also beliefs that have been programmed into us that we're not even aware of. And here's where our brain believes it's protecting us but it's also doing us a great injustice.

What happens is, we develop an irrational loyalty to our beliefs and we work hard to find evidence that supports these beliefs. We discard and avoid information that doesn't support them. Politics is such a great example of this. Think about how even more polarized we've become politically because everyone has gotten so attached to their beliefs. We don't seek out challenges to our beliefs. Instead, we prefer people and things that share our "enlightened" values. We like evidence that supports our pre-set world view. We often hold our beliefs more strongly after being presented with counter evidence. "Is that the best you've got"? "I must be right." We have an ego driven desire to prevail. Our brain distorts reality in order to save us from the ego destroying effects of failure and pessimism.

Why? Why does all this happen?

Because our beliefs become an integral part of who we are. To lose a belief, we lose a portion of our identity. Our brain embellishes, enhances, and aggrandizes us. It excuses our faults and failures. We require our specialness. We require reasons to feel hopeful, to have an identity, to believe there's a better tomorrow. And our brain will do everything it can to protect those feelings. Otherwise, why get up in the morning?

But in reality, we simply shouldn't believe everything we think. To protect our ego, our brain is:

- ➤ Emotional
- ➤ Immoral
- ➤ Delusional
- ➤ Pig Headed
- ➤ Secretive
- ➤ Weak Willed
- ➤ Bigoted
- ➤ Vulnerable
- ➤ And falsely optimistic about our abilities and future success

What can you do about this?

First, simply be aware of it. Don't be so bull headed that you believe that this may be true for everyone else but not you. It's true for you too. Become more aware of when your beliefs are hijacking your rational mind.

Second, questions are the answer. You need to continuously ask questions. Is this belief true? Why do I believe that? Is there any chance I'm wrong? How could someone else interpret this situation? Etc., etc.

So, the first lesson of effective mind management is awareness and questions. Quit believing that your reality is the only truth. It's merely your twisted representation of the truth. We know that will take a little while to sink in and your ego may never allow you to fully believe it. But it's true so we'll say it again. Your reality is merely a twisted representation of the truth.

Peak performers are much better at having relatively higher levels of awareness and a few less irrational moments. Be a truth seeker. Challenge yourself. Learn. Consider new ideas. Question your current points of view. By doing so, you take control of your mind vs. being controlled by it.

Behavior change is one of the most challenging aspects of being human. Let's not underestimate that. Frankly, immediate pleasure exerts a stronger influence on us than our long term well being. That's a big reason we don't change or feel unmotivated. Take our word for it, we'll find plenty of ways to rationalize our behaviors but again, reality is reality. We humans are not very good at delaying gratification or working through discomfort. We don't like it very much. But people who are at the top of their game have the ability to control their mind, thoughts, and emotions at a higher level. We can be a slave to our lizard brain or we can behave like a peak performer and manage our mind efficiently.

One of the other extremely important aspects of mind management is critical thinking.

Critical Thinking

Critical thinking is a type of reasonable, reflective thinking that is aimed at deciding what to believe or what to do. It is a way of deciding whether a claim is always true, sometimes true, partly true, or false.

Peak performers are often the best critical thinkers.

Why do we often not think in a critical manner and, instead, believe irrational things?

1.   We want to believe. Belief is the natural state of things, the default option.
2.   It makes us uncomfortable not to believe things. We have a "belief engine" wired into our brain.
3.   We are pattern seeking creatures. We have a need to connect the dots. This is known as association learning. Often it is useful. Often we make associations that don't exist.
4.   We have a tendency to find meaningful patterns in both meaningful and meaningless noise. We may believe a pattern is real when it's not and vice versa.
5.   When we feel out of control, we are more likely to see patterns where they don't exist.
6.   What we are thinking about influences what we tend to see.
7.   We have a tendency to believe in things bigger, more powerful, and more moral that will "rescue" us.

Why is critical thinking important?

Through critical thinking, we acquire a way of assessing and upgrading our ability to judge well. It enables us to go into virtually any situation and to figure out the logic of whatever is happening in that situation. It provides a way for us to learn from new experiences through the process of continual self-assessment. Critical thinking, then, enables us to form sound beliefs and judgments, and in doing so, provides us with a basis for a 'rational and reasonable' emotional life. Think about the impact that can have on your insurance practice. When we're acting "rational and reasonable", we make far better business decisions than when we're being irrational or applying poorly thought out opinions.

Critical thinking allows us to deal with situations in a non-emotional way. It prevents us from being taken advantage of. It provides more predictable outcomes.

How to be a better critical thinker

➢ **Step back and become an observer-**
  In order to asses situations critically you must make yourself as objective as possible. By separating yourself from the issue at hand you can weigh all of your available options and make better decisions.

➢ **Listen -**
  Instead of being the one to talk all of the time, take a moment to listen; we mean really listen to what someone is saying. Without taking time to listen you may not have your facts straight

from the beginning and no amount of critical thinking can right this error.

> **Be Critical! -**
Stop taking everything at face value and look for the motives. What makes someone do the things they do? Why did he/she just say that? What does this really mean? Do they have an agenda? How do they benefit by me believing what they are telling me? By continually asking yourself questions and analyzing situations you will become a better critical thinker.

> **Do the research.-**
When presented with an idea, study the research as far as you can. If a concept or idea is new to you, examine all sides of it. It's fun to believe certain things but that doesn't always make them true.

> **Examine the logic. –**
Is the idea that's being presented to me logical and reasonable? Or do I have to go on faith? What evidence is there to support this idea?

> **Be a truth seeker. –**
Read, learn, pay attention, question, observe.

In taking control of your mind, first be aware that your beliefs and ego have a stronger influence on your behaviors than you realize. And second, understand the importance of critical thinking in sound mind management. This is a topic we could write many chapters on. But the main point is to get you to be the proactive master of your mind, rather than an innocent bystander.

Spend a week just being an observer of your thoughts. Start to understand that you are not your mind. You are the controller of it, which is an entirely different perspective. You're the boss.

To help you clear the clutter and really gain control of your mind, we've stolen a few exercises from sports psychology that we find work amazingly well for other professions too. Use these to help you relax and stay focused. They will help you build your "mind management muscles" as you go along.

Mind Management Exercises

The skills of mental training we will discuss are of an all-inclusive nature. Each is distinct and specific but in turn closely linked to the other. You can use them every day in a way that is practical for you.

Need help with this?

We have some completed examples to act as your guide. Go to

http://mentalcompass.com/your-practice/

and they will be sent right to you by email.

Relaxation/Activation

The ability to be composed under pressure is a necessity. The difference between those at the top and those lower levels is the way in which nerves and fear are managed. It is all right to have "butterflies in your stomach" as long as they are flying in formation. The top business owners treat anxiety as a friend. It is great to be excited about the opportunity to compete. However, when these butterflies start to interfere with the performance, it is crucial to have ways to gain control instantaneously. Finding a balance between feeling overly energized and overly relaxed is a key concept in mental training.

Relaxation

In order to relax in the midst of a stressful situation, sometimes the simplest method can bring about the best results. Breathing properly is great place to start. Proper breathing comes from the diaphragm. Breathing from the chest and shoulder areas is often associated with increased muscular and mental tension. Once a relaxed breathing pattern is established, you can calm yourself even further by relaxing your muscles once group at a time. Breathing techniques are best learned in a quiet place, laying or sitting in a comfortable chair with you eyes closed. With practice, the same effect can be accomplished with your eyes opened in a busy, stressful environment.

 You can move through the exercise at a comfortable pace, taking plenty of time to modulate your breathing and moving slowly through a "1 to 10" count and perhaps even repeating it 2 or 3 times. After regular practice at a measured pace (5-15 minutes), you can practice moving through the"1 to 10" count quickly as a way of calming yourself in a situation where time is limited.

Close your eyes. Turn your attention to your breathing. Be an observer to the process of your breathing. And notice the way in which you breathe. Is it deep or shallow? Regular or irregular? Let your self come to a way of breathing that is deep, slow, and regular. You will find as you breathe in this way, you will quite naturally come to be comfortable, relaxed, and at ease. You will find that you may relax even further by focusing, in conjunction with your breathing, on the muscle groups of your body. Begin to count slowly from "1 to 10" focusing your attention in order on the muscle groups of your body. Breathe in, count"1" silently to yourself, focus your attention on the muscles in the abdomen, and when you breathe out let these muscles relax. (Repeat: 2-chest & shoulders, 3 neck, jaw, and head, 4 extremities). Once again, turn your attention to your breathing and let it be comfortable, relaxed and at ease. Count backward from "3" to "1" and open your eyes. When you open your eyes, allow yourself to remain relaxed and at ease. Relaxation can also be accomplished in variety of other ways, for example: listening to quiet music, focusing on something not related to your business, or finding a quiet place where you can simply retreat.

Activation

Relaxation gets our mind in a state that is calm and rational. It's difficult to engage in the best behaviors when we are wired and upset. We need calm rationality to take the best actions. This allows you to "activate" yourself in proactive ways that will move you forward, not just reactionary or whimsical actions. Proper relaxation leads to proper activation. Once you learn how to relax properly, you can begin to learn correct activation techniques. There are many variations and techniques on how to increase energy but the key to remember is when. The timing of your activation is crucial for whether or not you reach their optimal level of activation at the right moment. Some good activation exercise include listening to energizing music, reviewing competitive goals, and using imagery to imagine yourself performing at your highest level. Breathing can also be used for activation. The basic physiological concept here is that an increased rate of breathing will increase your heart rate. With increased activation comes other changes in body chemistry that can create an "adrenaline surge".

Concentration

Concentration is able to focus on the right thing, in the right way, at the right time. You must focus your attention on the task at hand and to not be distracted by internal (thoughts, feelings) or external (noise and other distractions from the environment) stimuli. Correct concentration cannot be forced, but learned as an acquired skill where in you remain in the present time, not thinking about the past or future.

Concentration Training

When practicing, make sure you are in a comfortable position.

1. For the next few minutes, take your self through the "Relaxation 1-10" exercise.

Once you are fully relaxed, proceed to the next step.

2. Now listen to what you hear by taking each separate sound, identifying it, and then mentally labeling it, such as voices, footsteps, or a cough. Next, simultaneously attend to all the sound

without attempting to identify or label them. You should listen to the mixture of sounds as you would music, while verbal thinking falls away.

3. Now become aware of bodily sensations such as the feeling of where the chair or floor supports your body. Mentally label each sensation as you notice it. Before moving on to another sensation, let each sensation linger for a moment while you examine it; consider its quality and its source. Next, feel all these sensations simultaneously without identifying or labeling any particular one. This compels you to go into the broadest possible internal body awareness.

4. Attend now only to your emotions or thoughts. Let each thought or emotion appear gently, without being forced. Identify the nature of your thoughts and feelings. Remain calm no matter how enjoyable or repulsive they may be. Feel one, then another, then another. Now try to tune into only one and hold your attention there.

5. Open your eyes and pick some object across the room directly in front of you. While looking ahead, see as much of the room and the objects in the room as your peripheral vision will allow. Simultaneously observe the entire room and all the

items in it. Picture now a broad funnel into which your mind is moving. Centered in the middle of the funnel is the object directly across the room from you. Gradually narrow your focus by narrowing the funnel so the only thing at the small end of the funnel is the object across from you. Expand your focus little by little, widening the funnel until you can see everything in the room. Think of your external focus as a zoom lens; practice zooming in and out, narrowing or broadening your focus according to your wishes.

Visualization and Imagery

Research has shown that the same neuro pathways in the brain are activated when you vividly imagine experiencing something as when you actually do it.

Using your mind to create an image of what you want creates a strong impression on the brain and helps improve performance and get results.

Athletes apply this principle when imagining having won a competition prior to the actual event. Olympic swimmers, like Michael Phelps, imagine themselves swimming with webbed hands and feet to improve their performance in the water.

Just as visualizing a desired result can produce results for athletes, it is a proven tool for success to build, boost and improve your business performance.

Remember: Visualization is not about seeing yourself trying to succeed at some point in the future. It is about picturing and experiencing, with the full resources of your imagination, your desired results accomplished in the present moment.

Visualization Tips:

When visualizing, it is important to view the action from the first person point of view. You experience yourself having achieved your goal through your own eyes, rather than watching yourself from the outside.

Adding kinesthetic (what you feel with your goal accomplished) and auditory (what you hear with your goal accomplished) dimensions enhance the process. Include in your visualization:

⇒ What you see, hear and feel with your goal accomplished.
⇒ What you are saying to yourself about accomplishing your goal.

⇒ Write your visualization – a scene that reflects your result accomplished. This allows you to be specific in describing your result. Seeing the words on paper can make more of an impact on your mind and emotions then just imagining the scene in your mind.

⇒ Most people find it easier to visualize with eyes closed to eliminate distractions and focus their attention inward on their desired result. Focus on one specific result at a time.

⇒ Your visualization can be long or short. There are no time rules, although the more senses activated while you visualize the more potent the impression on the brain. You only need to visualize for roughly 17 seconds at a time.

Assignment for the next 7 days: Only 20 minutes per day

⇒ Review and clearly understand your vision every day.

⇒ Question (as the observer) everything you are thinking about.

⇒ Practice mental exercises

⇒ Detach from outcomes

What Just Happened?

The "What Just Happened" exercise below is something we'd like you to do several times over the coming weeks. It will help you manage your mind and focus on events in a rational way.

When should you do this exercise?

After an event that:

- ✓ ***Involved a disagreement***
- ✓ ***Left you feeling negative***
- ✓ ***Made you mad***
- ✓ ***Left you uneasy***
- ✓ ***Caused you to beat yourself up***

Conflict doesn't always exist with others. Sometimes we experience conflict alone. For example: You cheat on your diet and decide that you are a failure who will never lose weight.

1. ***Describe a recent event? (Facts only)***
2. ***What is your interpretation/point of view of what occurred?***
3. ***What was the result of what happened? The situation may not be finalized yet, but what are the results to date?***

*Let's just for fun take a deeper look at the
situation. In other words let's dispute it.*

4. *Evidence to support and conflict your
    interpretation. Your point of view, their
    point of view, and other factors. Was
    there an overreaction?*

5. *Alternative explanations (when we have
    an experience, we sometimes choose to
    focus on one single point, usually the most
    dire or destructive aspect of an event, even
    though there were many contributing
    factors)*

6. *What is changeable in this situation?
    What are the specifics (unique factors),
    what are the non-personal aspects?*

7. *Implications, How likely is it?   is there a
    way to minimize the blow of the situation?
    In other words what is most likely, least
    likely, and middle ground?*

8. *Usefulness, (What good will it do to hold
    on to this?)*

9. *What can you do to make the best of this
    event? How can you use your strengths?*

Even though we only devoted one chapter to this subject, we think it's one of the most important aspects of being a high performance agent or broker. If you can manage your mind well, you're ahead of 90% of your competition.

Practice, practice, and practice this stuff. It will make a huge difference in your outcomes and general state of mind.

In the next couple chapters, we talk about relationship management, starting with the relationship with yourself.

CHAPTER 7 – MANAGING THE RELATIONSHIP WITH YOURSELF

Managing relationships is a key influencer on peak performance and being a high performance broker for several reasons. In order to be our best, we need healthy contact with ourselves, others, and our environment. We need others to help us reach our vision. Nobody ever does it alone. And we need a healthy relationship with our self in order to perform at our best.

In the next two chapters, we will discuss managing these relationships and the concept of well being.

Our relationship with our self

For many of us, the idea of having a relationship with ourselves sounds strange. But we have thoughts about ourselves, we have feelings about ourselves, and we talk to ourselves. We certainly spend a lot of time with ourselves. Thus, we have a relationship with ourselves. And this relationship is one of the most important we will ever have; it is fundamental to all other relationships. As the old cliché states, there's a reason that the flight attendant tells you that, in the case of loss of cabin pressure, put your oxygen mask on before you put your child's on. If you don't have at least a workable relationship with yourself, it is impossible to have workable relationships with others. Moreover, when we have a positive relationship with ourselves, others seem to respond and react accordingly.

We've seen a number of brokers who, after going through a bad spell, will consistently beat themselves up and blame themselves, treat their bodies and minds like crap, and generally see themselves as the problem. These are drastic cases, of course, but it happens. More often, it's on a smaller scale, where we just aren't feeling 100% confident or are feeling slightly disgruntled. We can actually change and improve the relationship we have with ourselves in a way that will increase our productivity and overall level of well being.

Our relationship with our self first starts with monitoring. Begin the habit of monitoring some key patterns:

- ➢ Your reaction to events and circumstances
- ➢ How you feel at any given moment
- ➢ Why certain people annoy you or rub you the wrong way
- ➢ What are your behavior patterns under certain circumstances
- ➢ What types of people am I intimidated by

➤ Where do I "shine"

Doing the "What Just Happened Exercise" (p. 81)
is useful in monitoring your key patterns.
Don't make yourself bad and wrong as you examine
each of these. Look at yourself more objectively.
Start to notice where the habits and patterns are
that may cause you to have a less than optimal
relationship with yourself. If there are aspects of
your habits and patterns that you see getting in the
way, begin to work on them.

The second aspect of managing your relationship
with yourself is to ask some specific questions:

➤ Am I truthful with myself (we discussed this in
mind management)?
➤ Am I often beating myself up for no good
reason?
➤ Do I make assumptions about people, events,
and circumstances
➤ Do I have integrity?
➤ How do others see me?
➤ Should I be taken seriously?
➤ Do I often manipulate reality/others?
➤ Am I too rigid?
➤ Do I enjoy my own company?

Again, if there are areas where you hear alarm bells,
make a concerted effort to work on those. We

can't tell you specifically how you should address each of those issues. It will be different for each individual. But truly take the time and answer each of these questions. We're often completely unaware of how we are being with ourselves and others. We've gotten so used to simply going through the motions with our relationships, including the one with ourselves, that we don't even notice the negative patterns that we've fallen into. As crazy as it may sound, your own self talk plays a major role in your outcomes.

A third aspect of managing your relationship with yourself is how you treat your body. Taking good care of your body is key. We break it down into 3 main components:

- ➢ Emotions
- ➢ Exercise
- ➢ Eating

We are not health and fitness experts. Examine exercise and eating more closely on your own. Find a diet and exercise regimen that are appropriate and effective for you. But by all means do it. If you are engaged in lousy eating and exercise habits, you simply won't be among the best. We need good health to perform at our very best. This isn't a joke. Study after study is showing how the amount of sleep we get, the amount of starches and sugars we eat, our lack of good proteins, etc. has an effect on our behaviors and our outcomes. If you are one of the many people that we know who barely gets 5 hours sleep, eats lousy, and never exercises, you simply can never reach the highest levels of your potential.

**Mind Management exercises come in handy here (pp. 72 – 80)

Emotions

There's a common myth in many self help programs; the myth that you should always feel positive, that you shouldn't experience negative emotions. We don't believe this is true at all. Negative emotions can serve a definite and productive purpose. They can serve as a warning. They can tell us when we're off course and also can serve as a counter balance, keeping us grounded.

5 reasons why negative emotions are not entirely undesirable:

1. Bad stuff happens and it's appropriate and normal for a response to these situations to include "negative emotions" (a lack of response including at least some negative emotion might be cause for a different type of concern)

2. Appropriate experiences of emotions such as fear and anxiety protect us from danger (without fear and anxiety, for example, we'd very likely do things that we shouldn't do...such as get too close to cliff tops or wander in to other dangerous contexts without taking adequate precaution)
3. Different types of "negative" emotions such as guilt and remorse help us learn where and when we've done the wrong thing (and then hopefully help us to make amends)
4. Without any dark, it's difficult or impossible to experience the light (so sadness, in a way, helps us to enjoy happiness)
5. We're human and we make mistakes; with mistakes comes regret and a whole range of other "negative emotions". But these need not be entirely negative experiences if we learn from these situations and become wiser, stronger, better etc.

The key is not to attempt to eliminate negative emotions. The idea is to manage emotions, not be managed by them.

➢ Start to believe that you can control emotions.
➢ Pay attention to your emotions. Focus on what is happening around you and pay attention to how you respond to a particular situation.

- Never ignore your emotions hoping the situation will go away.
- Realize that emotions are part of normal life. Some emotions in fact are critical to business success, i.e., enthusiasm.
- Determine the source of your emotion. Is the emotion caused by something that happened in the past or is it based on something real that's happening right now?
- Understand your emotions. Identify what triggers you, understand your responses and develop behaviors that allow you to be more objective.

Positive Emotions	Negative Emotions
Joy	Anger
Interest	Shame/embarrassed
Love	Contempt
Amusement	Disgust
Awe	Hate
Gratitude	Guilt
Hope/Optimism	Sadness
Pride	Fear
Inspiration	Overwhelm/Stress
Serenity/ Contentment	

- ➢ Acknowledge your emotions as legitimate. Wishing them away or denying their existence will not solve the situation or provide any learning.

- ➢ Maintain a Neutral body and voice. By keeping your body loose and your tone neutral, you are more likely to remain calm and view a situation objectively.

Again, please don't worry about trying to eliminate negative emotions. It's impossible and it's unnecessary. Simply start to notice which emotions you feel throughout the day. Marcial Losada came up with a simple way to measure called the Losada ratio. It's the ratio of positive emotions to negative ones. The general rule for good emotional balance is 3 positive emotions to one negative. Attempting to eliminate negative emotions is a fruitless effort. But keeping them in balance is perfectly within your reach.

The final aspect of managing the relationship with yourself that we'd like to bring up is the one that definitely sounds the most new-agey. When we first introduce this concept to people, their eyes roll back and they often start to have a seizure. It's met with a lot of resistance, with responses like "I'm busy running an insurance practice. I can't worry about this stuff". But once they buy in, it's a game changer. They discover that it makes a lot of sense. Ok, we gave you fair warning, right? This is the most new-agey thing we'll talk about. Just try it on for size.

It goes something like this…Typically, when we ask someone why they want to be a higher performing agent, broker, or advisor the answer is, "Because I'll make more money". If you ask why they want more money, the answer is, "because I can take care of my family, have a secure future, and live the life I want". When you boil it down even further as to why they want to do all of that, the answer is always the same…"because I'll be happy". It almost always comes down to creating a life that makes them happy. So far, so good?

That shouldn't really surprise you. We understand that everyone wants to make a good living, to be able to take care of their family and enjoy the finer things in life. Those are perfectly legitimate aspirations. But it seems that what we really seem to want the most is simply a life and circumstances that make us and the people important to us happy.

The problem is, happiness is difficult to measure. It's a little vague and really hard to define. Some people might try to describe happiness as a feeling. But in our opinion, those fleeting feelings are more just moods, not an accurate portrayal of someone's overall happiness. There are plenty of people that may seem gruff or as if they are often in a bad mood but they might be perfectly happy. But we thought it was important to be able to look at happiness in a more objective, measurable way.

Rather than use the word happiness, let's take a look at things more from the perspective of well being. We took another page from the positive psychology playbook in introducing the idea of well being. Dr. Seligman broke it down further by describing well being as PERMA.

P – Positive Experiences

E – Engagement

R – Relationships

M – Meaning/Purpose

A – Accomplishment

P: Positive Experiences: things that give you joy and comfort. Could be as simple as your morning cup of coffee, or as complex as taking the trip of a lifetime.

E: Engagement: engagement is about flow: time stops, the loss of self-consciousness during an absorbing activity. Engagement is different, from positive emotion; for if you ask people who are in flow what they are thinking and feeling, they usually say, "nothing." Martin Seligman Founder of PERMA and Positive Psychology says "I believe that the concentrated attention that flow requires uses up all the cognitive and emotional resources that make up thought and feeling."

R: Relationships: the relationship with yourself, and the relationships you have with others. Do you have the relationships that you need to get what you want (personally & professionally)?

M: Meaning; this is where having a vision is important. What is all this about? Why are you here? When we speak to a business owners, and she gives us that look or wants to avoid the question, we ask them, " why do you own this business and go through all the trouble and worry"? What does it all mean to you? Why do you do what you do?

A: Accomplishment; what have you completed? Sometimes we get that look, when someone doesn't think they have any. Accomplishments don't always mean money or big success. It's something that needed some effort to do. For example, a couple years back we hosted a TEDx event. This was a huge undertaking and wouldn't be complete for some time. Within that time, there were many accomplishments. Sometimes getting started is an accomplishment in and of itself.

The premise is that, if you pay attention closely to each of these 5 aspects of well being, you are highly likely to experience what you would describe as happiness. It's also an objective way to measure happiness or figure out what's wrong when things are off kilter a bit. There, that wasn't too new-agey, was it?

As a broker and trusted advisor, it's very important for you to have a healthy relationship with yourself. If you don't, people can smell it a mile away. They may not know exactly what it is, they'll just know that they don't necessarily want to do business with you. People want to work with a broker who seems confident, content, authoritative, and knowledgeable. A positive relationship with yourself is the key.

In chapter 8, we're going to dig into a subject that can dramatically increase your revenues in relatively short order. Even if you think you're already good at it, you can always be better. And that is...relationships with other people.

CHAPTER 8 – YOUR RELATIONSHIPS WITH OTHER PEOPLE

We're going to make a bold statement to start off this chapter. We said at the beginning that this isn't really a "how to" book. It doesn't teach specific topics like sales or management. But here's the bold statement. If you fully understand and apply the principles in this chapter, it will increase your sales more than any sales training ever will. We believe this to be 100% true and have witnessed it time and time again. When you effectively manage the relationships with others, they trust you. They believe you. They look to you as a resource. And they believe you have their best interests in mind. Unfortunately, a great deal of the sales training you've gone through is all about techniques. "If they say this, then you say that". "If they use this objection, then you use this reply." "Get an upfront contract". Get the point? Not all of these techniques are bad. Some of them can work when practiced over and over. But the most reliable way to increase your sales is not about techniques. It's about managing relationships and effective communication. What better way to create a new customer than for them to see you as a trusted advisor. We know you've heard it a thousand times. But we'll venture to guess that nobody has ever really explained this to you in a way that created any behavior change. We have a client that has worked with us for longer than any other client we have. He also happens to own a very successful insurance agency. In a recent conversation over lunch, he told us that if brokers really wanted to increase their sales, they would learn to take extremely good, extraordinarily good care of their customers. Yes, we all agree that everyone still needs to be engaged in constant sales and marketing activities. That isn't the point. The main point is that, being great at building relationships and communicating will be the greatest tool in your marketing bag. In our experience, if you lined up a hundred brokers and asked them how they stand out from their competition, 95 would answer "customer service". If that's true, why do the vast majority of consumers state that they feel neglected by their broker? The way to customer service is via creating a solid foundation of a relationship. One of the key factors in sales is the concept of likability. But likability doesn't simply mean being friendly or telling really good jokes. When people were asked to describe what they meant by likability, here were the most common answers:

- ➤ Connected – understands them
- ➤ Truthful
- ➤ Forthright/honest

➢ Says what they mean
➢ Follows through

In other words…they are really good at building relationships.

Managing the relationships with others isn't just about increasing your sales. There's a number of reasons why you want to become an expert at managing relationships. When people are in well-managed relationships they feel aligned, committed, on board and motivated. Their needs and wants are being considered; their quirks and individual ways of working are being accommodated; their contributions are being acknowledged. Communication seems to work effortlessly (we're going to talk a lot about communication in a few minutes).

Relationships with others are imperative to being a peak performer. As with the relationship with yourself, you simply won't be one of the top 1% without being able to have solid relationships with others. Why is this, you might ask?

The first is our need to be a part of a community. We humans thrive when we are part of a community. We feel connected, safe, and important. Without realizing, we continuously strive to be part of our various communities, whether personal or professional. We perform best when we are part of a community. We get a sense of comfort from it. So being an expert in relationship building increases your value in your various communities.

Also, no matter what our personal or professional vision is, it always takes other people. We rarely achieve our major goals without the help, connections, ideas, and input of other people. We can't think of everything on our own. Think about all the major accomplishments you've had in your life. How many of them did you achieve completely by yourself? We'll bet the answer is, "not many". We need others to help us carry out the mission.

Strong relationships with others helps us to express our ideas effectively and keeps our ego in check. They help us understand how we're being heard and seen by the outside world. Relationships with others can help us have a better relationship with ourselves. They can help us see our blind spots. Relationships with others teach us the rules of living that will help us in being our very best.

Now, there are a few myths about relationships with others that we'd like to bust. We won't spend a ton of time on them but they are important to mention.

Myths about relationships:

- ➢ Other people are the key to my happiness. – key distinction
- ➢ People love to do things exactly the way we think they should.
- ➢ You need a lot of intimate relationships to be happy.
- ➢ If I give in first, I'm weak.
- ➢ Strong relationships never have any secrets or separateness
- ➢ I have to oblige – can't say no

Being good at relationships with others does not mean being walked on, taken advantage of, manipulating others, or saying yes to everything. It simply means living in harmony with those who are important to us. It means working in a way with others that doesn't completely alienate them or make them want to not be near you. Our agendas are not all the same. That's ok. We're not the center of each other's universe.

In taking a closer look at your relationships with others, first take a look at what your responsibilities are in that relationship. Identify where your relationships with some important people may be lacking and what possible role you've played in the deterioration of the relationships. This is often the most difficult aspect of relationship management for people. Remember when we talked about ego protection? Our ego makes it very difficult to believe that we are ever the problem in a relationship. It actually warps our view of reality most of the time to make others bad and wrong. So please, first just start by being willing to be honest where you may need to take some responsibility for improving the relationship. It doesn't make you weak. It makes you a top performer.

Next, do an evaluation of which relationships are critical to the accomplishment of your vision. Obviously, we can't have a relationship with everyone. Start by focusing on the ones that are most important. What aspects of managing your professional relationships are most *important for you?*

- ➢ *Inspiration/*loyalty
- ➢ Influence
- ➢ Develop employees
- ➢ Initiate change
- ➢ Manage conflict
- ➢ Attracting/retaining key people

Proactively examine all of these aspects of your relationships. Don't just let them happen by accident.

What else can you do to create strong relationships with other people?

1. Build relationships one at a time. Fortunately or unfortunately, there are no short cuts. Sending out a newsletter helps you keep in touch with lots of folks, but it's no substitute for getting to know a real person.

2. Be friendly and make a connection. This may seem self-evident, but a friendly word or smile can make someone's day. Try to find something in common: all of us want to have close connections with our fellow humans.

3. Ask people questions. People love to talk about themselves and about what they think. If you ask people about themselves and then take the time to listen attentively, they can become your fast friend.

4. Tell people about yourself. People won't trust you unless you are willing to trust them. Tell them what you genuinely care about and what you think.

5. Go places and do things. When asked why he robbed banks, the robber replied, "Because that's where the money is." Go where the people are

6. Accept people the way they are. You don't have to agree with them all the time in order to form a relationship with them. No one likes to be judged.

7. Assume other people want to form relationships, too. Underneath the crabbiest looking person is often a lonely soul hoping someone will make a crack in their shell.

8. Overcome your fear of rejection. Most of us suffer from a fear of rejection, and there's only one thing to do about that: get over it. If you want to form relationships, plan on being rejected some of the time. You will be richly rewarded the rest of the time with the new relationships you have made.

9. Be persistent. People are often shy and suspicious. It takes a while to win trust. You can almost always form a relationship if you stick with it.

10. Invite people to get involved. People want to become part of something bigger than themselves. Many people are looking for an opportunity to meet other people who share common goals. At the worst, people will be flattered that you invited them to join.

11. Enjoy people. If you genuinely enjoy people, others will be attracted to your attitude. People will more likely want to be around you.

12. Engage in active listening. Take time to listen to what others are saying. Making assumptions on what you think people want can harm a relationship, and become frustrating for all parties involved.

➢ Ask questions
➢ Watch body language and facial expressions
➢ Watch for cues other than verbal
➢ Pay attention when someone is speaking. Don't use that time to plan what you are going to say next. (people notice this)

13. Acknowledge others. Noticing the little things or complimenting someone on a job well done goes a long way. It shows that you are paying attention. Engaging in this behavior also helps remove the awkwardness of negative feedback.

Interesting Fact: Most people spend 6 seconds or less complimenting others. Criticizing often takes longer than 6 seconds.

---

14. Watch your language. Being overly critical or complimentary can be harmful to a relationship. Trust is built when there is a healthy balance. A 3:1 ratio is recommended. Three positive comments to every negative one.

What else will help you create strong relationships with others? Read on...

What kind of communicator are you?

A very important component of relationships is our style of Communication. We can't begin to stress how important this is. This can make or break relationships almost in an instant. We promise we're not exaggerating. Sadly, we have known people in the past who have not paid enough attention to this.

 More often than not the frustration we feel when the people around us aren't "getting it" or cooperating is usually the result of a communication breakdown (and the fact that we don't like it at all when someone doesn't agree with us). EVERY time we speak, we choose and use one of four basic communication styles: assertive, aggressive, passive and passive-aggressive. In fact, we use all four in and out throughout the day, depending on what we believe will work best to get our needs met. Let's take a sneak peek inside each one of these styles and what makes them "tick" so that you can then use these clues to better understand and communicate with the people around you.

Aggressive communicators feel as though there is a winner and a loser in a conversation. Therefore, they come into the conversation with the expectation of winning and feel as though the only way they can do this is to overpower the other person

Passive communicators feel as though they need to keep peace in a conversation, and therefore, come into the conversation with the expectation of keeping the peace at all costs.

The Passive aggressive communicator is torn, they have a belief that peace needs to be kept at all cost, yet they resent this and therefore will leave the conversation feeling taken advantage of, and set out to win. Their winning is usually done in a quiet way that sabotages the situation, but doesn't implicate them.

The Assertive communicator believes they can best accomplish a task by clearly expressing their needs and what needs to get done. They do this in a way that doesn't attack or belittle the other. They have no expectation of how the other is going to react ahead of time. Their mission is to get the job done in a way that allows everyone to keep their dignity.

It would be unrealistic to say that we are one type of communicator all the time, because as you listen to each definition, you could probably identify situations where you have used all four styles of communication. That being said, there is probably one type of communication style that you fall back on more often than not.

So, how can you tell which type of communicator you are? The best and easiest way is to reflect back over recent conversations and pay attention to current conversations to replay how the conversation went. How did you speak to someone? How did they understand it? What were the outcomes? Did everyone walk away satisfied? Did you get what you needed from the conversation? This requires a very proactive, thoughtful method of communicating.

In our quest for peak performance, we have found that peak performers are assertive communicators. Because assertive communication meets our needs without having to use extra energy.

➢ Assertive communicators, don't get riled up before during and after a communication
➢ Assertive communicators don't take on too many projects that lead to either overload or letting others down.
➢ Assertive communicators don't spend their precious energy plotting and reliving the event
➢ And they don't use the time that should be spent on listening, thinking about what they are

going to say next . They spend that time listening to the other person.

They also:

- ➢ Get their needs met
- ➢ Use their time efficiently
- ➢ Engage in productive conversations
- ➢ And become peak performers

When you respect yourself to be assertive in your interactions you can leverage the best parts of a relationship.

So what do you do with this information?

1. Begin to pay attention to which communication styles you use throughout the day.
- ➢ How often do you use a communication style other than assertive?
- ➢ Watch and identify the communication styles some of the difficult people in your life use, and begin to notice how others use manipulative techniques to get their way.

This can be very confronting at first, but don't let it get you down. Knowing is step one.

2. Commit to becoming more assertive in your communication. This will be a work in progress,

take it day by day. You most likely won't knock it out of the park on your first day. If you have the will, then the rest is just practice.

People may not always know how to react if you are suddenly an assertive communicator when you may not have been one in the past. It may even confuse them a little. Don't let that stop you. People will get used to it and you'll find that it has a very positive effect on your relationships over time.

Now you may be asking Why do you want to take your time to do this? Things are fine the way they are, I am used to this way of interacting.

Think about this. How much energy do you used before during and after an interaction? Like everything we need to prepare, even if we are so used to it that we don't even notice.

Aggressive communicators get fueled by taking control. If you are focused on controlling the situation, it is difficult to properly listen. It's also difficult or intimidating to the other (especially the passive) to engage. You may get what you want, but are you really. By taking over the conversation you miss the benefit of the other side. The person or persons you are talking to want the time with you to be as short as possible, they aren't going to think of new ideas or participate fully. They will want to avoid you. Even if they are helping on a project, their focus is on making sure they are following your instructions, not on doing their best. They either can't or won't find a better way of getting the job done. The aggressive sucks the life out of a project, or relationship and that person is ultimately alone. If you are an aggressive, you probably feel like you are surrounded by idiots, and nothing gets done without you. You are probably exhausted.

Passive communicators are so worried about keeping the peace and making everyone happy that they suppress themselves. You don't ever speak up even when you know you have the better idea, and you hardly ever get what you want, because you don't want to inconvenience anyone. You may tell yourself that you enjoy making others happy, and it doesn't matter. This may be true some of the time, but more often than not, your passivity or niceness is not real, its done out of habit or fear. By communicating this way you lose your self slowly. In addition to what you are doing to yourself, you lose the respect of the people around you. You are the person that people get to dump their stuff on. You never have an opinion. You give up your credibility every time you choose the passive route. You can't nice your way to the top. Passives get passed over. You also, never fully participate in a conversation. Instead of actively listening, you are concerning yourself with anticipating what the other wants to hear, and missing most of the conversation.

Passive Aggressive communicators have it the worst, and coincidently are the most damaging kind. They suffer the consequences of the passive and the aggressive. You get walked on, and people are repelled by you, because they are listening to your endless complaining and blaming. Your aversion to confront the appropriate person in the right way leads others to distrust you. They can't help but wonder what you are saying about them, and when they will be next on your chopping block. You are constantly feeling frustrated, angry, and fearful. Frustrated that you are being taken advantage of. Angry, because you aren't getting what you think you deserve, and fearful because you don't know how to say what you mean. You started out as a passive, pleasing people is all you know. Yes I said it watch out Passives, keep it up long enough and you end up like this. And forget about your ability to listen! You have the angel and devil on your shoulder at all times, you can barely hear a word anyone is saying. If you do manage to hear a word, you put so many stories and meaning around it, that you usually miss what they are trying to say.

We can't stress enough the importance of Assertive communication. You can't become a peak performer without it. Start slowly, make the commitment. The will, commitment and practice will get you there.

The real point of this chapter is that if you want to increase your sales, improve your customer service, have more productive employees, and have more satisfying personal interactions, then pay extremely close attention to building relationships with other people.

CHAPTER 9 – THE TRUTH ABOUT GOAL SETTING

There are very few things in management literature, business coaching, self-help books, and consulting mentioned more often than setting goals. We're sure you've heard them described in different ways...SMART goals, big hairy audacious goals, stretch goals. We're also sure that you've been taught over the years to create goals that are somewhat out of your reach. The bigger the better as far as goals are concerned. Well, as it turns out, that is not always the best advice. In fact, it's almost never the best advice. We promised at the beginning that we'd be turning some of the conventional wisdom on its head. This is one of those times. We need to have a serious talk about goals. The right goals can definitely drive productive behavior and increase business performance. The big question, though, is when to use goal setting, how often, and in what circumstances. The truth of the matter is that goal setting is an over-prescribed activity that can potentially cause harm to a business organization. Goal setting should be done quite selectively, on a limited basis, and carefully monitored. The evidence shows that the harmful side effects of goal setting are far more serious and widespread than most insurance brokers realize. Goal setting can undermine performance, cause us to focus on the wrong things, harm relationships and culture, demotivate us, and be the root of risky or even unethical behavior.

Without question, every organization must continually explore new ideas, innovate, research, and have strong objectives. We need to always be thinking about what the possibilities are for our organization. We need to position ourselves well in the short term while never losing sight of creating long term value and continuity.

Understanding Goals

Under the right circumstances, at the right time, with the right company, the right people, and the right resources, goal setting can be a powerful tool. Stretch goals can shift thinking, reenergize an organization, prompt innovation and learning, and enhance performance across all levels of the organization. Ironically, companies that are in the best position to achieve stretch goals almost never set them, while companies that have experienced recent failures and have a "nothing to lose" attitude are almost always more likely to set big goals.

Sadly, the struggling companies are actually the ones that should avoid setting big goals completely. It almost seems backward but read on...

"As goals become extreme, there are complex yet predictable organizational effects that are likely to be negative except under a limited set of specifiable circumstances" (Sitkin, See, Miller, Lawless, Carton 2011).

One of the first ways that goals can inhibit our results is a phenomenon known as "inattentional blindness". With goals, we tend to narrow our focus. This narrow focus can often cause us to ignore other important issues that are not related to the goal. So while we may actually accomplish the goal, it often becomes apparent that other aspects of our businesses or lives suffer because of it. Insurance practices see this happen in a number of ways; shoddy products or services, a decline in service, unhappy customers, etc. As business owners, we need to continuously be aware of how every aspect of our business is functioning. A major goal that we are hyper focused on will often impede the way we process information and inhibit our ability to learn. For a major goal where the achievement of it is not well understood and there aren't specific, concrete steps to reach it, we can become disorganized and impulsive due to focusing too much attention on the goal. This hyper vigilance on the goal can also lead us to focus too much energy on outside ideas or quick fixes. As we've all experienced, quick fixes never turn into a solid long term solution.

In our experience and research, we've found that stretch goals can be devastating to motivation, morale, and performance. When we don't have a clear set of steps to reach a particular goal, a sense of fear or helplessness can set in. We will often start to see a seemingly impossible goal as unrealistic and we can quickly lose our commitment to the goal and our desire to pursue it. We have seen this happen countless times with brokers and advisors. Someone convinces them that they should be setting huge, lofty goals that are out of their reach and abilities. Although the people giving this advice have likely never achieved any of their own stretch goals, it's in vogue to offer such advice. And what happens? Nothing. People quickly lose interest and find tons of reasons why they couldn't pursue that particular goal at this time. Less extreme goals that are difficult but still attainable are much more advised. Stretch goals that don't come to pass are a common source of poor morale in a person or an organization. Many well-meaning people claim that there is a correlation between the level of difficulty of a goal and a boost in our performance. This is not necessarily true. Goals should be at a high enough level of difficulty to inspire innovation, energy, commitment, and motivation. However, when they are out of our current reach and ability level, there are some significant psychological costs related to failing to reach a goal. In pursuing a stretch goal, there is likely vague guidance at best. This affects coordination and performance and can leave people with a difficult time coping and a loss of intrinsic motivation.

As we alluded to prior, stretch goals will often lead businesses to adopt riskier strategies or take gambles that they shouldn't. There are glaring examples of this that we're all familiar with, i.e. Enron, the Ford Pinto, a number of banks, the mortgage meltdown, you name it. But don't think that this type of risky behavior is reserved only for large companies. We've observed it many times with very small companies as well. The long term results are always the same. This risky type of behavior can also lead to competition and a lack of cooperation within an organization.

Things to consider

Two major areas that we need to consider when deciding what goals to pursue are recent performance and available resources. Studies out of Harvard, Duke, and other major universities have shown that companies that are in the best position to set and reach goals are companies that have had recent success stories and have the available resources to pursue the goal. When we speak of resources we mean money, people, information, knowledge, and skill. When an organization has had a recent history of success, this is a great time to go after larger goals and objectives. Success breeds success. It's been shown countless times that the best time to stretch ourselves even further is after a recent "win". Moreover, with the available resources behind us, they can act as a physical and psychological buffer against potential failures (which there will continue to be many). If a person or company has experienced recent setbacks, they will be far better served by going after smaller wins, rather than the brass ring. It's vital to future performance.

Pursuing Goals

So how should you know what goals to pursue and when to pursue them?

First, decide if the goals are too specific. Make sure that goals are comprehensive and include all vital areas of the business. We want to avoid inattentional blindness.

Also, make sure that goals are challenging but not out of reach. We need to be sure that everyone involved in pursuing the goal has the knowledge, skill, training, and experience that will allow the company to reach the goal. If not, the goal is likely going to have detrimental effects on morale, motivation, and performance across the board.

Make sure that the goals have real meaning and will cause you to be intrinsically motivated to achieve them. When goals are set for the wrong reasons or by someone else, they almost always have a negative effect on a person or business.

It's also helpful to set learning goals rather than performance goals. We've seen that when an agency sets a goal like reaching $1,000,000 per year in revenue, they are far less likely to reach them vs. someone who has created learning goals, goals that are completely within their control, and personal performance goals.

Make sure you question whether or not a goal could potentially cause you to engage in risky or unethical behavior. This needs to be constantly monitored, as it can sneak in to our behaviors without us realizing it. Understand what the potential negative side effects of the goal are.

Make sure that goals are geared toward your current level of ability or the ability of the organization. As counterintuitive as it may sound, attempting to stretch beyond what we are capable of is more often than not a recipe for failure and demotivation.

Finally, take a close look at your recent success, failures, and available resources. If you have had recent setbacks, you need to set yourself up with some smaller wins before going after the loftier goals. The psychological benefits are huge. If you are on a roll, it's a time to look at bigger goals. And be realistic with yourself in regard to the resources that are available to you in pursuing the goal. If you don't have the proper resources, the goal is likely not to come to fruition.

Goal setting is not a panacea and if not done properly can cause serious harm to an organization of any size. On the flipside, it can be a great motivator and source of innovation. Make sure you're setting them in the right way and always handle them with care.

We don't want to discourage you from setting goals or thinking big. That's not the idea at all. The main point we want you to take away from this chapter is that goal setting is not something you should do whimsically or without the proper foundation behind them. Create sensible goals that build upon one another and cause you to have to increase your skills. You'll achieve far better results both short term and long term rather than setting huge goals that you have no idea how to accomplish.

In the next chapter...if it doesn't get measured, it doesn't exist.

CHAPTER 10 – PERFORMANCE BASED MEASUREMENT, DAILY & WEEKLY ACTIVITIES, TRAINING YOUR BRAIN FOR PEAK PERFORMANCE

Admittedly, this might be the most dry chapter of the book. We apologize in advance. It can't all be fun and games. We'll try to make it as entertaining as possible though. We're also going to combine several topics into one chapter, as they are all related to one another. We'll make it all weave together nicely for you. As dry as this might be, it's important stuff. We wouldn't bring it to you if it wasn't important, right?

A mentor of ours that we worked with a long time ago had a favorite phrase. He'd like to say "if it doesn't get measured, it doesn't exist". Over the years, we have found this to be completely true. If we don't measure our progress and compare it to where we thought we would be, how do we really know how we're performing? Sure, you might look at your financial statements once in awhile or meet with your accountant once or twice a year but are you really measuring your progress on a regular basis? Most people are not. This is one of the biggest causes of stagnation and missed goals. We simply aren't paying attention. We have a good friend who's been a business owner for nearly 15 years. He's not in the insurance world. He's in technology. But a few years after he launched his business, we were having a beer one sunny Friday afternoon and he turned to us and said "I've never really looked at the numbers in any meaningful way. Today I did...and I realized that all I've done is create a low paying job for myself". From that moment on, things changed. He redefined his target market. He got clarity and focus on his product line and his pricing. And he put the right priorities in place that caused him to grow at a faster rate and nearly doubled his profit margin. All of this came out of taking the time to look at what was really going on. It was a huge amount of change that he put his business through. It probably wouldn't have happened if he didn't take the time to measure where he was.

Up until now, this book has been ideas and concepts at more of the "30,000 foot view". We've introduced some big ideas at a macro level. Now it's time to get down to the micro level. It's time to roll up your sleeves and get into some details. It's also time to hold yourself accountable to some specific outcomes, which you are going to outline over the course of this chapter. The first key in measurement is to identify what your priorities in your own practice are. These may differ from person to person and from practice to practice. The way you will define and measure your priorities are what we call Performance Based Measurements (PBM's).

We know it sounds like a big, scary phrase that is probably way too complicated to be useful, right? Good news. PBM's are not complicated at all. In fact, once people understand and buy into this concept, we've seen PBM's become an integral part of their practice. So what are they? PBM's help you define and measure progress toward your bigger vision. Once you are crystal clear on what your vision is, on exactly what it is you'd like to accomplish, you need a simple, pragmatic way to measure progress. Performance based measurements are that method. PBM's are quantifiable measurements that you decide on that reflect the critical success factors of your practice. They'll differ depending on the organization. Maybe a few examples of what we're talking about will help:

A business might have as one of its PBM's the percentage of its income that comes from return customers. Obviously, it's more desirable and less costly to a business to have a high retention rate. So measuring that rate helps them clearly understand how their customers feel about them.

Do you think this can affect their long term vision? Of course.

A school may focus its PBM's on graduation rates of its students.

A customer service department might have as a PBM the percentage of customer calls that are answered in the first minute.

A PBM for a social service organization might be the number of clients assisted during a calendar year.

You probably get the idea now. Whatever PBM's you select, they must reflect your goals and vision, they must be key to its success, and they must be measurable, i.e., number of new policies written, etc. Again, think of PBM's as your priority items that will tell you if you are moving closer to or further away from your vision. For example, if one of your long term goals is to work less hours (we have many clients with that goal), then a PBM for you would be the number of hours you work per week. They should also be behavior based, meaning they are controllable by your own behaviors, not highly affected by the outside world. In other words, outcomes that you personally can be held accountable for. As our friend Jim would say, PBM's are a way to decide "who's going to do what by when".

Performance Based Measurements Must be Key To Reaching Your Vision. Many things are measurable. That does not make them key to your success. In selecting Performance Based Measurements, it is critical to limit them to those factors that are essential to the organization reaching its goals. It is also important to keep the number of Performance Based Measurements small just to keep everyone's attention focused on achieving the same PBMs.

What Do I Do With Performance Based Measurements?

Once you have good Performance Based Measurements defined, ones that reflect your vision, ones that you can measure, what do you do with them? You use Performance Based Measurements as a performance management tool. PBMs give everyone in the organization a clear picture of what is important, of what they need to make happen. You use that to manage performance. You make sure that everything the people in your organization do is focused on meeting or exceeding those Performance Based Measurements. Post the PBMs everywhere: in the lunch room, on the walls of every conference room, on the company intranet, even on the company web site for some of them. Show what the target for each PBM is and show the progress toward that target for each of them. People will be motivated to reach those PBM targets.

In our experience, PBM's have several positive aspects:

They help you understand and focus efforts on your top priorities.

They help you outline your specific goals and action steps.

When monitored on a regular basis, they help you measure progress toward your vision.

Our suggestion is that you don't gloss over this. We understand that measurement is easy to let slip through the cracks. But don't. If you don't track your progress, how will you know how you're doing? Our guess would be that 90% or more of the brokers that we've met don't use anything similar to PBM's. And sadly, the vast majority of brokers are making nowhere near the money they'd like. Being like the 90% is easy. Tracking progress and taking appropriate corrective action when needed is something that the very few but most successful do. Who's results would you rather get?

So it's highly likely that you are now asking yourself, "is there an easy way to track this? It seems like it could be complicated." Lucky for you we've put together some great templates for daily and weekly activities. You may want to make several copies of each of these so you never run out.

Daily and Weekly Activities for Ongoing Peak Performance

Training Your Brain For Peak Performance

Powerful ways to keep your brain healthy and performing at a peak level:

➤ Aerobic exercise – walking, jogging, swimming, elliptical, etc.

➤ Drink plenty of water – proper hydration keeps your brain functioning properly

➤ Eat plenty of whole grains, omega 3 vitamins and beans

➤ Eat breakfast every day

➤ Drink moderately – 2 to 3 per day for men, 1 to 2 per day for women

➤ Read a good book – reading stimulates brain activity, imagination, and creativity

- ➢ Get plenty of rest
- ➢ Maintain positive focus and thoughts toward achieving your vision
- ➢ Constantly be learning
- ➢ Get romantic (especially if you're a woman)
- ➢ Break your routines – drive to work a different direction – change things up
- ➢ Work with numbers
- ➢ A little less television
- ➢ Expand your vocabulary
- ➢ Practice recalling memories in detail

Need help with this?

We have some completed examples to act as your guide. Go to
http://mentalcompass.com/your-practice/
and they will be sent right to you by email.

Daily Review

---

1. What were my top objectives for today?

2. What did I accomplish today?

3. What did I anticipate well today?

4. What did I fail to anticipate?

5. What did I learn today?

6. As a result, what changes have taken place in my mind-set, knowledge, game plan, and execution skills?

7. What additional assistance do I need to succeed?

Knowledge/Information:

- ✓ Feedback:
- ✓ Support:
- ✓ Resources:

Weekly Peak Performance Checklist

Please rate your behavior (from 5 to 1) on the following 10 questions:

5 -- Never

4 -- Not Much

3 -- Sometimes

2 -- A lot

1 – Always

1. **I seem to be rushing through things. _____**
2. **I tend to alternate between working on two or more equally unpleasant tasks. _____**
3. **I feel fatigued a great deal of the time. _____**
4. **I experience more slack periods of non-productive activity than I can afford. _____**
5. **I constantly miss self imposed   deadlines. _____**

6. **I find myself pushing back self imposed deadlines. ____**
7. **I have insufficient time for rest or sleep. ____**
8. **I have insufficient time for personal relationships and recreation. ____**
9. **I feel overwhelmed by demands and/or details. ____**
10. **I feel that I spend my time having to do what I don't want to do. ____**

Total ____

SCORING:

45-50 High Score(Peak Performer)
38-44 Above Average: Needs fine tuning, doing well but inconsistent
23-37 Moderate: Functional, consistently not reaching potential
16-22 Below Average: Marginal - needs considerable work
10-15 Danger Zone – Take immediate action

Weekly PBMs and Goals Review

Performance Based Measurements the specific "pieces" that you will measure when working toward your vision.

What are your PBM's?

Are you taking action toward each of your PBM's daily?

If no, why not? What is preventing you from focusing on your PBM's?

What knowledge, skill, resources, or information are you lacking that are necessary in your PBM's?

Goals – Review your Goals weekly

Visionary or long-range goals are the ones that seem a long way off and difficult to achieve. They may be anything from six months to several years away.

Intermediate goals are benchmarks for where you want to be at a specific time, as they relate to your Performance Based Measurements. For example, intermediate goals may include revenue, number of clients, key actions or behaviors, etc.

Short-term or daily goals are the most important because they provide a specific focus for our ongoing training. Past research on business has found that setting daily goals was one factor that distinguished successful business owners from their less successful counterparts.

Are you on track with each of your goals?

Do you have the necessary knowledge, resources, skill, information, and environment to reach your goals?

Are they realistic?

PBM Exercise

Vision Restated:

_____

_____

_____

Performance Based Measurements Relevant to Achieving Vision:

_____

_____

_____

Specific goals that need to happen to achieve PBM's:

_____

_____

_____

Top Priorities:

First PBM to address:_____

_____

First goal to address:_____

_____

Immediate next steps:

_____

_____

_____

_____

Existing business defects that could inhibit vision:

_____

_____

_____

_____

Bad habits/flawed thinking that could inhibit vision:

_____

_____

_____

_____

_____

_____

_____

The key point to remember from this chapter is that, if you don't track, measure, and make continuous adjustments, you will be like a rudderless ship being taken wherever the current wants to take you. Use this chapter as a set of tools to make those measurements and adjustments. In the next chapter, if there are two things you can do to dramatically increase your revenue, these are it…

Chapter 11 – Coaching and Mentoring for a Better Insurance Practice

In this chapter, we're going to go into two areas that we think are crucial to being a high performance broker. You've heard the phrase many times that "no man is an island". No woman either, for that matter. So we're going to present two concepts here that we strongly encourage you to consider, a peer advisory board (sometimes known as a mastermind group or Roundtable) and a highly qualified coach.

Harness The Power of an Advisory Board

We have a former client. Let's call him Waldo (boy will he be mad when he finds out we called him Waldo in the book). Waldo was not in the financial services world but his story will still resonate. Waldo had been an executive at a fortune 500 corporation for many years. Then he started a business consulting firm. He was also a long time member of one of our Roundtable groups. We asked him one day outright why he participates in a peer advisory board. He had such a vast array of business experience and business acumen and it made us quite curious what he got from it. We thought his answer was perfect. He said, "Have you ever watched somebody come up with a great idea or implement a great strategy and you said to yourself, why didn't I think of that?! Well, we simply can't think of everything. But when I'm in my Roundtable, someone has already thought of it, experienced it, messed it up, did it well, and earned valuable wisdom to pass on to others. I don't have to reinvent the wheel". That's exactly what your board will do. They'll provide you many beneficial answers and insights you wouldn't have discovered on your own.

No business is too small or too large for the owner to benefit from an advisory board. An advisory board is such a powerful management tool that no business owner should be without. To be competitive and profitable, your practice needs to be hitting on all cylinders. We have yet to meet a business owner that is an expert in all areas of his business and few with the resources to hire experts and consultants.

Moreover, we have discovered that the answers to all business challenges lie within the business owner. A quality advisory board will help elicit those answers and move a business forward. In fact, a study from the Small Business Administration showed that, between 2001 and 2004, business owners with an advisory board grew 44%, while those without one grew 25%.

Think about the last time that you met with other business people and had an open discussion, sharing your ideas and concerns. An advisory board is a formal version of this process. It's been said that we can share 90% of our business life with almost anyone. It's the other 10% where a trusted group of advisors can make an enormous difference. Trust, integrity, and mutual respect are the keys to a valuable advisory board.

Unlike a one-time or casual event, your advisory board should be composed of people with a genuine interest in your business, and you in theirs. A desire to see each board member gain clarity will benefit every member of the board. Your advisory board should serve as a sounding board as well as a source of ideas, expertise, and experience. More than anyone else, your advisory board will be on your side and you on theirs. They are people with no agenda and no axe to grind that will want to contribute to the well being of your business. No single person can know everything, and "on the fly" advice can often be worse than no advice at all. An advisory board that meets regularly gets to know you and your business in an intimate way and can help you find new ways of thinking and the ability to face various challenges.

But the best aspect of an advisory board is that you can share ideas, concerns, and challenges in a safe, non-judgmental environment with those who are your peers. You will be able to enlarge the view of your business and improve your mission and strategy. You will have new ideas that you hadn't considered before and gain the ability to measure if you are on the right path or may need to change direction. The bottom line is that you will get better results in a shorter period of time.

For an advisory board to provide a high level of quality to busy business owners, it must possess 4 basic components:

- ➢ A working agreement among the board members along with a memorandum of understanding and procedure.
- ➢ Confidentiality agreements signed. (Imperative as to not compromise the integrity of the group)
- ➢ Commitment to being active in the group.
- ➢ An agenda (This will keep the meetings from losing direction and lowering the quality)

An advisory board should aim to have every member of the board commit themselves to supporting, sharing experience with, and respecting all of their fellow board members. Well run advisory boards are truly the secret to running a successful business, even when the business is already successful in its own right.

You will see dramatic improvement in your business when you participate in a well run advisory board. Don't isolate yourself and convince yourself that you know everything and have no defects. When talking with your advisory board, you will often discover something that was hidden within you until that moment. Let's face it; the top is a lonely place sometimes. Business owners often have few ways to get support and guidance. Your employees expect you to have all the answers, but where can you turn when you need help with those answers? That's where an advisory board can make all the difference. Think of your advisors as mentors who help you become a more effective business leader. They inspire you to greater leadership heights through their own examples and experiences. They help you get through the tough times. They support and encourage. An advisory board can bring out the best in you.

The old African proverb states, "it takes a village to raise a child". No man, woman, or family is an island unto itself. We venture into a new role, undertake a new project or set out to do what no man has done before. Whatever direction we choose to take, we go there with limited knowledge and experience. "The Village" can take many forms, but the one commonality is we seek the knowledge of those who have come before us.

Entrepreneurs are a proud and independent group; we have a better way and are willing to assume all the risk to deliver our product to the world. Unfortunately, pride and independence can work for us and against us at the same time. An entrepreneur is someone with the courage and passion to take a concept and turn it into a business and is willing to do whatever it takes to achieve his or her desired outcomes. Entrepreneurs can also restrict themselves to solitary confinement and resist the aid of "the village".

Why do we resist?

- ➢ Fear of looking bad in front of others
- ➢ Need Permission
- ➢ Didn't know the option was available – never heard of it
- ➢ Waste of time (we think)
- ➢ Don't know who to ask about it

For us personally and professionally, "the village" has become our own greatest resource. The residents of our village are fellow entrepreneurs who have shared with us their experiences and expertise. In return, we gave them the gift of our experience and expertise. Our mastermind group has become the governing branch of our village. They have shared with us their experience, supported us when we have fallen, been patient, and never judgmental. They have helped us to align ourselves with our business, take leadership, and look at the business for what it is and what it can become.   We all posses the power to accomplish what we set out to do, some take the long route and others seek the direct route. When we accept the village we remove the fear, and isolation that can stunt our progress. Think of your mastermind group as your village, your "go to" resource when you need clear perspective and the truth.

Now let's spend a few minutes talking about coaching. We've met a number of people who were reluctant to hire a coach. They weren't sure exactly what they would get out of it. After all, every minute you're not making a sale is a minute that you're not making a sale. We've found in working with our private clients that coaching has some distinct and very real benefits though, benefits that can improve your sales for sure. Frankly, coaching works because it brings out your best. Good executive coaches believe that the best answers already lie within you. They work with you to discover those answers, clear the head trash, and stay on track. A good coach also helps you hold yourself accountable to results!

Specifically, here are some things that your coach will do for you: first and foremost, listen. Your story is central to the process, how you're feeling, how you're responding and engaging. Your coach will look at all of these. Your coach will fully engage in what you're saying. Your coach will listen carefully and provide constructive feedback and observations based on what they've heard.

Also, your coach will ask you a lot of questions. Coaches use questions to stimulate your thinking and creativity. They ask you questions about your goals, your decisions, your behaviors and activities, what's possible, and your future. They'll help you take a close look at every aspect of your business and life and keep them firing on all cylinders. Your coach will also encourage you. Everyone needs some encouragement from time to time. We probably don't get nearly enough. Your coach will help you recognize your vision, your progress, and your efforts. The coach will also facilitate while letting you lead. They will facilitate your learning and problem solving but they are never fully leading. You are. It's all about your agenda and your approach.

The reasons that people use coaches are endless and unique to each person. But here are a few of the reasons that we've found that people use a coach:

- ➤ When they need to make significant changes
- ➤ To deal with uncertainty more effectively
- ➤ To make better decisions
- ➤ To set better goals
- ➤ To reach goals faster
- ➤ To become more financially stable
- ➤ To make a bigger impact
- ➤ To be a better leader
- ➤ To simplify their lives
- ➤ To reduce stress
- ➤ To keep up with a very fast paced industry
- ➤ To get out of their own way

There are probably a hundred more good reasons to work with a coach. But here's the bottom line, whether you decide to work with a peer advisory board, a coach, or both, please don't be an island. Other people will stimulate your thinking and prevent you from believing your own b.s. too. We've seen it with dozens of business owners of every walk of life, when they become part of an advisory board or hire a coach, their results increase in real and sometimes dramatic fashion. People often describe their Roundtable as their oasis, where they can step away from the day to day fires and take a bigger picture view of their practice. If you don't already work with a board or coach, we highly suggest you make that a priority item. The time and effort is well worth it.

There are organizations you can go to for this type of help (us being one of them) or you can form your own informal advisory board. But however you go about it, just do it.

Chapter 12 – Summing It All Up

We know that we've covered a lot of ground throughout this book. There's quite a bit for you to absorb. We understand. Don't try to soak it in all at once. Come back and refer to the book as many times as you need to. It's a long journey that we're all on. Don't try to make all your changes in one day. We hope this becomes your reference guide for turning your practice into precisely what you want it to be. It's quite possible. We've seen it happen many times.

Once in awhile, you'll feel discouraged. It's ok. Things don't always happen when we want them to or exactly in the way we wanted them to. As we're sure you've heard many times before, nothing worthwhile comes easy. Peak performance is a lifelong journey. That being said, it's not as daunting as you might think. We know we have already said it a few times throughout the book but there is one point that we want to emphasize one more time. Just make one better decision every day. Absorb and understand the concepts that we've presented to you and use them to make one better, more proactive decision every day. Take one better action each day. Control your mind a little bit more each day. Improve one thing about your relationships every day. If you follow this philosophy, you will be amazed at the speed with which changes begin to take place.

You'll find that working toward being a high performance broker can be extremely enjoyable and rewarding. That's our goal for you. We don't want you to enjoy it "someday". Make that day be today. There seems to be a misconception that people have adopted over time...that it takes drudgery and misery to reach the highest levels of performance. We're here to tell you that it's not true. You can become a peak performer and enjoy the process. In fact, we'd go so far as to say that, if you are not enjoying the process at all, you are doing something wrong or may have chosen the wrong field. You'll find the work you put in to be intensely rewarding. The sense of real satisfaction and pride that you'll have will propel you to even higher levels.

So don't gloss over the material. This is definitely not a race. We want you to adapt these concepts to your everyday life and the operation of your practice. It will take time and effort. There's no doubt that old habits are terribly hard to break. Be patient with yourself along the way. You're not searching for miracles. Please remember, you just need to be a little bit better than you were yesterday.

We wish you the utmost success on your journey. We know that you have it in you to be a high performance insurance broker. Hopefully, this book has helped coax out a little bit more of your own internal greatness. If things still aren't 100% clear or if you're left with some questions, please don't hesitate to reach out to us. You can find us through our website at **www.mentalcompass.com** or just send us an email to **info@theecircle.com.**

In 2014, we'll be releasing our audio course called *How To Be a High Performance Insurance Broker.. The Step by Step system to turn your Insurance Practice into a High Revenue Generating Machine.* The program will go into a bit more detail around each of the subjects we've presented. So keep your eyes and ears out for that program.

We know this isn't easy. That's why there are so few people at the very top. If there are two traits that we think are completely necessary for peak performance, they are resilience and courage. It takes both to be the best. Most people aren't cut out for it. But that's good news for you. It's perfectly within your reach to be at the very top of your field, one of the elite. Don't give up. When you persevere and keep striving, you'll make it. There's no doubt.

Thank you for allowing us to be part of your quest to be a high performance insurance broker

Resources

RECOMMENDED READING

Authentic Happiness by Martin Seligman. This is the first book to outline the VIA Classification and many key theories and principles of positive psychology (e.g., the pleasure, engagement, and meaning pathways to authentic happiness).

Character Strengths and Virtues by Chris Peterson and Martin Seligman. (a bit dry, very scientific)

Flow by Mihaly Csikszentmihalyi

Start with Why by Simon Sinek

Man's Search for Meaning by Viktor E. Frankl

The Book on Mind Management by Dennis Deaton

Learned Optimism by Martin Seligman.

Coaching the Mental Game by H.A. Dorfman

Positivity by Barbara Frederickson

Thick Face Black Heart by Chin Ning Chu

Life Would be Easy if it Weren't for Other People by Connie Podesta

The Science of Getting Rich by Wallace D. Wattles. (Free PDF download on internet)

Principles by Ray Dalio (Free PDF download on internet)

Flourish by Martin Seligman

The Happiness Advantage by Shawn Achor

LINKS

Character Strengths Assessment
www.viacharacter.org

Understanding Positive & Negative Emotions www.positivityratio.com

Martin Seligman Positive Psychology
www.pursuit-of-happiness.org

Losada Ratio
www.losadalineconsulting.net/#!losadaline
/c5ro

Jennifer Rizzotti
www.hartfordhawks.com/coaches.aspx?pa
th=wbball&rc=228

Alex Linley (Linley et al., 2010)
http://positiveacorn.com/wp-
content/uploads/2012/01/Linley_2010.pd
f

Sitkin, See Miller, Lawless, Carton 2011
http://cole.fuqua.duke.edu/research/pape
rs/Sitkin%20et%20al%20%20%28AMR%2
02011%29.pdf

Inattentional Blindness
www.scholarpedia.org/article/Inattentiona
l_blindness

ACKNOWLEDGEMENTS

There are many people that helped make this book a reality. We want to take this opportunity to thank our "Village".

A special thank you to Minds in Motion and Women Wisdom (Armen, Bill, Brent, Carolyn, Jenn, Lynn, Steve, Terry, Tim & Yvonne). Thank you for believing in us, and your continued support. Your conversations and successes have been an inspiration.

To Noris our oldest (not in age) and most loyal client, who always believed in us.

To Frank, Vickie, Martin & Norma for providing us roots and wings.

Parker and Greg, you took a chance, your faith in our ability has not gone unnoticed.

To Jody for giving us a chance

To Bob, thanks for your support, wisdom, and mentorship

To Jenn & Mike, you have both been so gracious with your time, wisdom, and knowledge.

To Dave who stood up and took notice.

To Travis for holding Mike accountable

Thanks "Sista Mary" for being the teacher that you are.

And finally, a special thank you to all members of The Entrepreneur Circle, past and present. You have all given us a gift, whether it a lesson, an opportunity to improve, or just the chance to have a new relationship, we couldn't have done it without the experience.

ABOUT THE AUTHORS

Maria and Mike Keiser are the co-founders of The Entrepreneur Circle, an organization that offers peer advisory boards, coaching, and peak performance training to insurance brokers, agents, and other financial services entrepreneurs. The work they do provides brokers with a set of tools that help them reach their highest levels of performance. They have been working with financial services entrepreneurs for more than 10 years. They are devoted to teaching others how to think, speak, and behave like a peak performer. Their goal is to help be the very best in their field.

The Keisers have been business owners since 1997 and use their business knowledge and experience to assist their clients in building profitable and valuable practices. They very much believe in the philosophy of "practice what you preach".

They have spent years researching, practicing, and perfecting the concepts that are discussed in "Your Practice By Design". Many people have described their work as "innovative and refreshing" because of the fact that everything they present is practical, pragmatic, and useful in the everyday operation of your practice. None of it is "pie in the sky" theory or just old ideas you've heard before.

Their tools are based on the work they've been doing with private clients as well as exhaustive research and practice. The Keisers definitely take conventional wisdom and turn it on its head. But their feeling is that they would much rather provide information to readers and clients that actually works, rather than drudge up the same old status quo.

This book will challenge you, make you think, inspire you, and hopefully cause you to take the appropriate actions and engage in the behaviors that lead to a high performance insurance practice.

Want More?

We hope you have enjoyed this book, it is our hope that the information provided for you helps you become your best self. All it takes is desire, commitment to yourself and making one better decision each day. Use this book as a guide, make notes, fold down pages, and refer back to it often. The best compliment would be to see thousands of tattered copies.

If you enjoyed this book and want to continue the journey with us you can:

- ✓ **Subscribe to our Podcast**
- ✓ **Subscribe to our mailing list**
- ✓ **Attend a Peak Performance Training Live Class**

www.mentalcompass.com

Need help with the exercises?
Go to **http://mentalcompass.com/your-practice/**
Coming Soon

The On-line Course "How to Become a High Performance Insurance Broker...The Step by Step System to turn your Insurance Practice into a High Revenue Generating Machine"

As always feel free to drop us a note info@theecircle.com.

24536761R00093